taste.
INDIAN

Over 100 mouth-watering recipes

igloo

igloo

Published in 2010
by Igloo Books Ltd
Cottage Farm
Sywell
NN6 0BJ

www.igloo-books.com
Copyright © 2010 Igloo Books Ltd

10 9 8 7 6 5 4 3 2
ISBN: 978 1 84852 838 3

Food photography and recipe development: Stockfood, The Food Image Agency
Front and back cover images © Stockfood, The Food Image Agency

Printed and manufactured in China.

contents.

introduction.

Our modern understanding of Indian food is as meaningless for Indians as their understanding of European food. The Indian subcontinent consists of several nations and covers 1.7 million square miles. India itself is made up of 35 states and territories inhabited by 1.8 billion people of many different races and religions. So it is no surprise that the foods cultivated, cooking traditions and styles vary considerably from region to region.

As well as differing geography and climate, other factors have contributed to the diversity of Indian food, such as the influence of neighbouring or invading cultures, from the Ancient Greeks, Persians and Mongols to, more recently, the British, Portuguese, French and Dutch. Religion also plays a major part, with the Hindus, Buddhists and Jains, for instance, developing vegetarian traditions to suit their beliefs, with considerable use of dahl, dishes of spiced pulses like chana (chickpeas) and masoor (lentils).

What really distinguishes Indian food, and characterizes it for Westerners, is its resourceful and inspired use of spices, from pungent mustard seeds to the subtly perfumed cardamom. Great use is also made of chillies, but not all Indian food is chilli-hot. Some dishes may contain only one spice, while others, particularly meat-based, may be flavoured by a dozen or more. Great skill lies in the subtle blending of a variety of spices to enhance rather than overwhelm the other flavours.

Although many religions coexist in India, the two that have most influenced its food are the Hindu and Muslim faiths. The Hindu vegetarian tradition is widespread in India, although today many Hindus eat meat, while the Muslim tradition is most evident in meat dishes. This is especially evident in the cooking of the Punjab region, which now straddles the Indian/Pakistani border in the North West. Punjabi food is what is most often found in Indian restaurants in the West and is largely based on the food of the Mughlai, the Persian–influenced cooking of the Moghul emperors who ruled most of India before the British. It includes kebabs, rich kormas (curries, for examples, see pages 64 and 112) and koftas (meatballs), biryani (layered rice and meat dishes, see pages 138 and 160), rogan josh (deep-red aromatic curry of goat, mutton or lamb, see page 82), and preparations from the clay oven or tandoor like tandoori rotis (thick flatbreads) and tandoori chicken, etc. Milk is also very important, in its many forms, such as dahi (yoghurt), lassi (a spiced yoghurt drink), Paneer (curd cheese) and ghee.

Ghee is a clarified and concentrated form of butter widely used in cooking. If you can't find it in the shops, just melt some butter gently in a heavy-based pan and then increase the heat until it is simmering gently and foaming on top. Continue in this way until it turns a good golden colour - anything from 10 to 45 minutes, depending on the butter's water content. Strain out the milk solids that have formed before use.

Goan food is influenced by the cooking of the Portuguese empire and makes much use of seafood. Perhaps its most famous type of dish is the fiercely chilli-hot vindaloo (see page 106). The food of the colder northerly province of Kashmir is rich and warming, seen in its korma dishes, usually based on mutton. Gujarati food is primarily vegetarian and is noted for its chaats or savoury snacks, such as bhel puri, (puffed rice and potato in a tangy tamarind sauce) now sold at the roadside stalls all over India, as well as its sweet curries like dhansak, made from lentils, cumin, ginger and garlic, and either gourd or pumpkin, to which the Parsi community (descended from the Persians) add mutton.

South Indian food, particularly that of the Tamil Nadu province, is best-known for its idlis (lentil and rice cakes), dosas (crisp savoury pancakes) sambhar (tamarind-flavoured vegetable stews) and vada (pulse- or potato-based 'dougnuts'). The mostly vegetarian food of the South uses generous amounts of spices and coconut. Rice is very much the staple food, rather than the wheat-based chapatis, rotis and parathas (flatbreads) favoured in the north (see our rice and breads section). The south is also the origin of many of the sweet dishes favoured all over India, such a kheer (spiced rice pudding) and kulfi (spiced ice cream). Throughout India meals are often rounded off with paan, or betel leaf wrapped around an assortment of digestive spices like aniseed, cloves and cardamom.

The excitingly varied recipes that follow are carefully designed to give you the true flavor of this wonderfully diverse type of cooking. Arranged in chapters on Starters & Sides, Meat and Fish Dishes, Vegetarian Dishes, Rice & Bread and Desserts, these recipes offer readers the ability to prepare interesting, authentic and tasty Indian food to suit any type of occasion, from family meals to special occasion celebrations and dinner parties.

starters
& sides.

Tamarind and date chutney with poppadoms

Prep and cook time: 1 hour 40 minutes
Cannot be frozen
Serves: 4

Ingredients:
For the chutney:
40 g | 3 tbsp tamarind paste
200 g | 1 ⅓ cups dried dates, stones removed, roughly chopped
½ tsp ground cumin
juice 1 lemon
Cayenne pepper

For the poppadoms:
3 ½ g | ½ tsp dried yeast
250 g | 2 cups plain|all purpose flour
½ tsp salt
5 tbsp olive oil
1 tsp ground cumin
sea salt

Method:
To make the chutney, mix the tamarind paste with 100 ml / ½ cup hot water and allow to rest.

Place the dates, cumin, lemon juice, salt and Cayenne pepper in pot with 100 ml / ½ cup water and bring to a boil. Stir in the tamarind paste and strain. A paste should be left in the sieve. Let cool and season with salt and Cayenne pepper.

To make the poppadoms, mix the yeast with 100 ml / ½ cup lukewarm water until smooth.

Mix the flour, salt and 3 tbsp olive oil in a bowl and add the dissolved yeast. Knead into a soft dough. Add a little more water if the dough is too dry. The mixture should not stick to the bowl. Cover and allow to rise in a warm place for 1 hour until the dough is twice its original size. Mix the cumin with the remaining oil.

Re-knead the dough on a floured work surface and roll into a cylinder, 5 cm / 2" diameter. Cut into equal pieces and using lots of flour roll the pieces into very thin circles 10 cm / 4" diameter.

Heat a large non-stick skillet (not too hot) and fry the poppadoms one after the other on both sides for 1-2 minutes until crispy. Brush with the cumin-oil and sprinkle with sea salt and let cool on a wire rack. Serve with the chutney.

Vegetable samosas

Prep and cook time: 1 hour 30 minutes
Cannot be frozen
Serves: 4

Ingredients:
For the raita:
1 onion, finely grated
½ cucumber, finely grated
300 g | 1 ¼ cups yoghurt
1 tbsp sugar
juice of 1 lemon
1 pinch ground cumin

For the samosas:
50 g | 2 tbsp ghee
250 g | 2 cups plain|all purpose flour
2 cardamom pods, seeds removed
2 tsp brown mustard seeds
1 pinch turmeric powder
300 g | 2 cups potatoes, diced
2 garlic cloves, chopped
75 g | ½ cup frozen peas, defrosted
2 tbsp fresh coriander|cilantro leaves
oil, for frying

To garnish:
fennel seeds
mint

Method:

To make the raita, mix the onion and cucumber in a bowl and season well. Allow to rest for one hour. Then rinse with cold water and drain well.

Mix the yoghurt with the sugar and lemon juice. Add the onion-cucumber mixture and season with ground black pepper. Add some salt and the cumin and pour into bowls. Sprinkle with fennel seeds and chill. Before serving garnish with mint.

To make the samosa dough, heat half of the ghee and let cool slightly. Mix in the flour, salt and 120 ml / ½ cup water until a smooth dough is formed. Wrap the dough in foil and allow to rest for 30 minutes.

Grind the cardamom seeds and the mustard seeds using a mortar. Melt the remaining ghee in a pot and fry the cardamom and mustard seeds and the turmeric. Add the potatoes and the garlic and fry lightly.

Add 120 ml / ½ cup water, season with salt and allow to cook on a low heat for 10 minutes. Add the peas and cook for a further 5 minutes until the potatoes are soft. Stir in the coriander/ cilantro leaves and let cool.

Divide the dough into 8 pieces and roll out 15 cm (6") squares. Spoon some of the filling onto the middle of each square. Brush a little water on the edges of the dough squares, fold in half diagonally to create a triangle and pinch the edges closed.

Heat sufficient oil in a deep skillet (or a fryer) to 175°C (350°F) and deep-fry the samosas until golden brown. Pat dry with kitchen paper and serve hot with the cold raita.

Tandoori chicken kebabs

Prep and cook time: 40 minutes Marinade: 12 hours
Cannot be frozen
Serves: 4

Ingredients:
4 chicken breasts, skinned and cut into bite-size pieces
1 lemon, juiced

For the marinade:
200 g | 1 cup yoghurt
2 tbsp vegetable oil
¼ tsp ground cumin
¼ tsp ground nutmeg
¼ tsp ground coriander
¼ tsp black pepper
¼ tsp paprika
2 garlic cloves, crushed
1 tsp fresh ginger, peeled and grated

For the raita:
1 cucumber, grated
250 g | 1 ¼ cup yoghurt
1 tbsp parsley, finely chopped
1 tbsp mint, finely chopped
½ tsp ground caraway
½ tsp ground coriander

To garnish:
mint leaves

Method:
Place the chicken pieces in a flat dish. Season with salt and ground black pepper and drizzle with lemon juice.

To make the marinade, mix together the yoghurt, oil and the spices. Add the garlic and ginger. Generously brush the chicken with the marinade and cover the dish with tin foil. Marinate overnight in the refrigerator.

To make the raita, mix the cucumber with the yoghurt, parsley and mint and season with caraway, coriander, salt and ground black pepper. Allow to steep for 1 hour. Garnish with mint leaves.

Skewer the chicken pieces onto kebab sticks, reserving the marinade. Grill or bbq the kebabs for 8-10 minutes. Halfway through, turn and brush with the reserved marinade. Serve the tandoori chicken kebabs with the raita.

Curry soup with pineapple

Prep and cook time: 45 minutes
Can be frozen
Serves: 4

Ingredients:
1 tbsp ghee
1 onion, diced
1 tbsp curry powder
1 tsp turmeric
1 small fresh pineapple, diced,
1/3 set aside
1 apple, sliced
1 banana, sliced
4 tbsp coconut milk
500 ml | 2 cups chicken stock
250 ml | 1 cup milk
1 chicken breast, diagonally sliced
4 tbsp almonds, chopped and roasted
naan bread, to serve

Method:

Heat the ghee and fry the onions. Add the curry powder and turmeric and cook for 10 minutes.

Add the fruit and fry together quickly. Add the coconut milk, stock and the milk, bring to the boil and then simmer for 15-20 minutes.

Remove from the heat and puree with a hand blender.

Add the chicken and the remaining pineapple to the soup and simmer for a further 3-4 minutes. Season with salt.

Pour the soup into bowls, sprinkle with almonds and serve with naan bread.

Vegetable pakoras

Prep and cook time: 1 hour 30 minutes
Cannot be frozen
Serves: 4

Ingredients:
150 g | 2 cups gram (chickpea) flour
50 g | 6 tbsp plain|all purpose flour
1 tsp baking powder
2 tsp salt
1/4 tsp turmeric
1 tsp garam masala
1 tsp ground coriander
1 tsp chilli powder
200 g | 1 ¼ cups waxy potatoes, cut into bite-sized cubes
150 g | 1 cup cauliflower florets
150 g | 1 cup broccoli florets
200 g | ¾ cup aubergine|eggplant, thinly sliced
1 onion, sliced
oil, for frying
sweet chilli sauce, or chutney

Method:

Mix the gram flour, plain/all purpose flour, baking powder and spices (salt, turmeric, garam masala, coriander, chilli powder) in a bowl, add 300 ml / 1 ¼ cups water and whisk to a smooth batter. Leave to stand for about 30 minutes.

Parboil the potatoes for about 10 minutes, then drain. Blanch the cauliflower and broccoli in plenty of boiling water for 3 minutes. Drain, refresh in ice-cold water and drain thoroughly.

Heat the oil (it is hot enough when bubbles form on the handle of a wooden spoon dipped into the hot oil). Dip the aubergine/eggplant, onion, potatoes, cauliflower and broccoli pieces individually into the batter and fry in the hot oil, in batches, until golden brown.

Drain thoroughly on absorbent kitchen paper and serve with sweet chilli sauce or chutney.

Lentil balls with coconut chutney

Prep and cook time: 45 minutes
Cannot be frozen
Serves: 4

Ingredients:
250 g | 1 ¼ cups red lentils, washed
2 shallots, roughly chopped
2 garlic cloves, roughly chopped
1 red chilli pepper, seeds removed,
cut into strips
1 green chilli pepper,
seeds removed, cut into strips
1 tsp fennel seeds
1 - 2 tbsp flour
1 tsp baking powder
vegetable oil, for frying

For the coconut chutney:
1 shallot, diced
150 g | ⅔ cup yoghurt
100 g | 1 ¼ cup desiccated coconut
1 tbsp fresh coriander|cilantro
leaves, chopped
2 - 3 tsp sesame oil
chilli powder

To garnish:
coriander|cilantro leaves

Method:
Cook the lentils in boiling water for 15 minutes until al dente. Drain and let dry.

To make the coconut chutney, puree the shallot, yoghurt, coconut and coriander/cilantro and stir in the sesame oil. If the chutney is too firm stir in a little hot water. Season with salt and chilli powder and chill in the refrigerator.

Place the lentils in a deep bowl. Add the shallots, garlic and chillies and puree using a hand blender. Stir in the fennel seeds and salt. Add the flour and baking powder until a kneadable dough is formed.

With damp hands shape the dough into small balls. Heat the oil in a pan (you can tell when the oil is hot enough as bubbles appear on a wooden spoon dipped in the hot oil). Fry the lentil balls for 4 minutes until golden brown. Pat dry using kitchen paper, garnish with coriander/cilantro leaves and serve with the coconut chutney.

Momos – steamed dumplings with a meat filling

Prep and cook time: 1 hour 55 minutes
Can be frozen
Serves: 4

Ingredients:
For the dough:
500 g | 4 cups plain|all purpose flour
1 tsp salt
1 tbsp vegetable oil
extra flour, to work with

For the filling:
350 g | 1 ½ cups beef, fillet or loin, finely chopped
1 garlic clove, finely chopped
1 onion, finely chopped
1 spring onion|scallion, finely chopped
2 cm | 1" fresh root ginger, grated
½ tsp garam masala

Method:

To make the dough, knead together the flour, salt, oil and 175 ml / 1 cup lukewarm water. Cover and allow to rest for 1 hour.

Mix the meat with the garlic, onion and spring onion/scallion and season with salt and garam masala. Add the ginger.

Make 12-16 small balls out of the dough and roll out on a floured board into thin circles.

Place 1 tbsp of the filling in the middle of each one. Fold the edges inside and press together.

Place the momos in a greased colander and steam for 15 minutes over a pot of boiling water. Serve with chilli sauce.

Chilled yoghurt soup with fresh mint

Prep and cook time: 15 minutes Chill: 30 minutes
Can be frozen
Serves: 4

Ingredients:
500 g | 2 cups yoghurt
250 ml | 1 cup cream
450 ml | 2 cups vegetable stock
½ tsp cumin
1 tbsp mint, chopped
lemon juice

To garnish:
sprigs of mint

Method:
Mix the yoghurt with the cream and gradually add the stock.

Add the cumin and the chopped mint and season with salt, ground black pepper and lemon juice.

Cover and chill in the refrigerator for 30 minutes.

Puree quickly, season and serve garnished with mint.

Potato bhajis with papaya chutney

Prep and cook time: 1 hour
Cannot be frozen
Serves: 4

Ingredients:
For the chutney:
2 tbsp ghee
1 green chilli pepper, finely chopped
1 pinch turmeric
1 tsp mustard seeds
2 tbsp brown sugar
2 green papayas, peeled, halved,
seeds removed and diced
1 lemon, juiced
1 tbsp fresh curry leaves, chopped

For the bhajis:
125 g | 1 ⅔ cups gram (chickpea) flour
¼ tsp baking powder
1 pinch ground turmeric
1 pinch Cayenne pepper
1 pinch coriander powder
1 tsp salt
½ tsp cumin
500 g | 1 ¼ lbs potatoes, thinly sliced
vegetable oil, for frying

To garnish:
curry leaves

Method:
To make the chutney, heat the ghee and sweat the chilli. Add the turmeric, mustard seeds, sugar and papaya, cook for 1 minute then add 120 ml / ½ cup water. Simmer for 10 minutes and then season with lemon juice, curry leaves and salt. Cool.

To make the bhajis, mix the gram flour with the baking powder, turmeric, Cayenne pepper, coriander powder and salt. Add the cumin and 250 ml / 1 cup water and stir into a thick liquid dough. Stir in the potato slices.

Heat the oil in a pot (you can tell when the oil is hot enough because bubbles will appear on a wooden spoon held in the oil). Fry each potato slice for 4 minutes until golden brown, turning occasionally. Pat dry on kitchen paper.

Quickly fry the curry leaves in the hot oil and use to garnish the bhajis. Serve with the papaya chutney.

Mango salsa

Prep and cook time: 20 minutes
Cannot be frozen
Serves: 4

Ingredients:
2 mangoes, peeled and diced
4 cloves
2 ½ cm | 1" fresh ginger, peeled
and grated
1 tsp brown sugar
juice 1 lemon
2 tbsp fresh coriander|cilantro
leaves, chopped
Cayenne pepper

To garnish:
coriander|cilantro leaves

Method:
Mix together the mangoes, cloves, lemon juice, sugar and chopped coriander/cilantro and allow to rest for 30 minutes for the flavors to fully develop.

Season with salt and Cayenne pepper and serve in small bowls garnished with coriander/cilantro leaves.

Parsnip soup and naan bread

Prep and cook time: 2 hours 15 minutes
Can be frozen
Serves: 4

Ingredients:
For the naan bread (makes 8):
150 ml | ⅔ cup milk
7 g | 2 tsp dried yeast
1 tsp sugar
500 g | 4 cups plain|all purpose flour
1 tsp salt
1 tsp baking powder
2 tbsp oil
150 g | ¾ cup natural yoghurt
1 egg
1 - 2 tbsp rosemary, finely chopped

For the soup:
40 ml | 8 tsp olive oil
2 onions, finely chopped
3 garlic cloves, finely chopped
1 tsp ground cumin
2 tsp rosemary leaves, chopped
500 g | 4 cups parsnips, diced
600 ml | 2 ½ cups vegetable stock
60 g | 1 cup green or black
olives, chopped

Method:
Heat the oven to 220°C (200°C fan) 425°F, gas 7.

To make the naan bread, heat the milk gently in a pot and crumble in the yeast. Add the sugar, stir well and allow to rest for 10 minutes until the yeast has dissolved.

Sift the flour into a large bowl, add the salt and baking powder and mix together. Add the milk-yeast mixture, oil, yoghurt and egg and knead into a dough. Cover and allow to rise in a warm place for 1 hour.

Knead the dough on a floured work surface, divide into 8 pieces and roll into balls. Roll 4 of the balls into teardrop-shaped naans and sprinkle with rosemary.

Place the naans on a cookie sheet and bake in the middle of the oven for 8 minutes until light brown. Prepare the remaining pieces of dough in the same way.

Heat the oil and fry the onions. Add the garlic, cumin and rosemary and cook quickly together.

Add the parsnip, then the stock and simmer for 30 minutes. Stir in the olives and then puree everything and season with ground black pepper.

Pour into bowls and serve with the hot naan bread.

Onion bhajis

Prep and cook time: 40 minutes
Cannot be frozen
Serves: 4

Ingredients:
2 onions, sliced into very thin rings
2 green chilli peppers, deseeded,
finely chopped
$\frac{1}{2}$ tsp chilli powder
2 tbsp fresh coriander|cilantro leaves,
finely chopped
3 tbsp lemon juice
1 tsp cumin seeds, roughly crushed
125 g | $\frac{1}{2}$ cup gram (chickpea) flour
2 tbsp water
1 pinch salt
500 ml | 2 cups sunflower oil,
for deep-frying

To garnish:
4 sprigs coriander|cilantro

Method:

Mix the onions and chilli peppers with the chilli powder, cilantro/coriander, lemon juice and cumin.

Stir the gram flour and salt into the onion mixture. Add the water and mix well. Season with salt.

Heat the oil in a pan (it is hot enough when bubbles form on the handle of a wooden spoon held in the oil). Take small balls of the onion mixture with a teaspoon and fry in the hot oil, a few at a time, until golden. Drain on paper towel and keep warm in the oven 70°C (60°C fan) 160°F, gas 2.

Serve at once, garnished with coriander/cilantro leaves.

Cheese and broccoli tikkis

Prep and cook time: 30 minutes
Cannot be frozen
Serves: 4 (8 tikkis)

Ingredients:
250 g | ½ lbs potatoes, cooked
and mashed
300 g | 4 cups broccoli florets
125 g | ¾ cup onions, finely chopped
2 garlic cloves, chopped
1-2 green chilli peppers, finely chopped
2 - 3 tbsp cornflour|cornstarch
70 g | ⅔ cup cheese, finely grated
100 g | 2 cups breadcrumbs
1 tbsp oil
oil, for frying

For the yoghurt sauce:
300 g | 1 ¼ cups natural yoghurt
1 tsp tandoori masala spice mix

Method:
Heat 1 tbsp oil in a skillet and cook the onions and garlic. Add the broccoli and fry for 4-5 minutes.

Season with salt, stir in the cornflour/cornstarch and cheese and let cool. Then mix with the mashed potatoes.

Divide the mass into 8 equal portions and shape into round cakes. Roll in the breadcrumbs and fry in a large skillet on both sides until golden brown.

Stir the masala spice mix into the yoghurt and serve alongside the tikkis.

Lamb samosas and tomato raita

Prep and cook time: 1 hour Chill: 2 hours
Cannot be frozen
Makes: 14 samosas

Ingredients:
For the samosas:
250 g | 2 cups flour
1 tsp salt
5 tbsp oil
2 onions, diced
2 garlic cloves, diced
1/2 red chilli pepper, finely chopped
2 tsp ground ginger
2 tsp madras curry powder
1/2 tsp ground coriander
1 tbsp lemon juice
250 g | 1 1/4 cups lamb fillet, diced
1 tbsp tomato puree
1 tbsp fresh mint, chopped
1 egg white
oil, for frying

For the tomato raita:
250 g / 1 cup yoghurt
100 g / 1/2 cup tomatoes, diced
1 tbsp onions, diced
1 tbsp fresh coriander|cilantro
leaves, chopped
1/4 tsp cumin powder

Method:

Mix the flour and salt on a work surface. Add 2 tbsp oil and 60 ml / 1/4 cup warm water and knead into a smooth dough, gradually adding 50 ml / 2 tbsp water to the mixture.

Wrap the dough in foil and allow to rest for 2 hours in the refrigerator.

Heat 3 tbsp oil in a skillet and sweat the onions and garlic. Add the chilli, ginger, curry powder and coriander and fry for 1 minute. Add the meat, lemon juice and 150 ml / 2/3 cup water and simmer on a low heat until the liquid has evaporated. Add the tomato puree and mint and then let the filling cool.

To make the raita mix the yoghurt with all the other ingredients and season to taste.

Re-knead the dough, halve it and roll one half out on a floured work surface to 20 x 42 cm (8" x 16.5") and cut out 7 strips 20 x 6 cm (8" x 2"). Do the same with the other half of dough.

Place a tsp of filling on one end of each strip and fold over diagonally so that the filling rests in the fold. Keep folding the dough strip along the diagonal until you get to the end. Brush the short end of the strip with egg white and press firmly closed.

Heat sufficient oil in a fryer or a skillet and deep fry the samosas (The oil is hot enough when small bubbles appear on a wooden spoon held in the oil). Serve with the tomato raita.

Potato pakoras with yoghurt sauce

Prep and cook time: 1 hour 30 minutes
Cannot be frozen
Serves: 4

Ingredients:
450 g | 1 llb potatoes
75 g | 1 cup gram (chickpea) flour
40 g | ¼ cup cornmeal
1 tsp fennel seeds
3 green chilli peppers, seeds removed,
finely chopped
2 tbsp coriander|cilantro leaves,
chopped
1 large onion, finely chopped
sunflower oil, for frying

For the yoghurt sauce:
200 g | 1 cup Greek yoghurt
1 tsp sugar
1 pinch salt
1 tsp fresh coriander|cilantro
leaves, chopped
1 tsp fresh mint leaves, chopped

Method:
Cook the potatoes in salt water for 30 minutes and then mash.

Mix the gram flour, cornmeal and the fennel seeds in a bowl.
Stir in the chilli, coriander/cilantro and onion.
Then add the potatoes and as much water as necessary to
form a thick, kneadable dough.

Heat the oil in another pot (you can tell when the oil is hot
enough as bubbles appear on a wooden spoon held in the oil).

Drop golf ball-sized portions of the dough into the oil and fry
until golden yellow. Pat dry on kitchen paper.

To make the yoghurt sauce simply mix all of the ingredients
together and season to taste. Serve the potato pakoras with
the yoghurt sauce.

Okra pods with onions

Prep and cook time: 30 minutes
Cannot be frozen
Serves: 4

Ingredients:
500 g | 5 cups okra pods, diagonally sliced into bite-size pieces
juice 1 lemon
3 onions, cut into rings
3 tbsp oil
50 ml | 10 tsp vegetable stock

Method:
Place the okra pods in a bowl with water and lemon juice.

Heat the oil and fry the onions on a high heat until brown. Add the okra pods and cook for 2 minutes.

Add the stock and allow to cook for 7 minutes. Season to taste and serve with naan bread.

Fried cauliflower with saffron

Prep and cook time: 20 minutes
Can be frozen
Serves: 4

Ingredients:
1 large cauliflower, divided into florets
4 tbsp ghee
1 pinch ground saffron
2 garlic cloves, finely chopped
4 cm | 2" fresh ginger, cut into thin strips
1 tsp cumin
2 green chilli peppers, seeds removed,
cut into fine strips

Method:
Blanch the cauliflower in salt water for 2-3 minutes then drain.

Heat the ghee in a large skillet and fry the saffron, garlic, ginger, cumin and chilli for a few minutes. Add the cauliflower and fry gently for 10 minutes, stirring occasionally.
If necessary add a little water but make sure it has all evaporated at the end.

Season with salt and ground black pepper and serve in bowls.

Saag mirch – spiced spinach with chilli peppers

Prep and cook time: 30 minutes
Cannot be frozen
Serves: 4

Ingredients:
2 tbsp ghee
2 red chilli peppers, split lengthwise and seeds removed
4 cm | 1 ½" fresh ginger, peeled and finely chopped
1 onion, chopped
1 - 2 tsp coriander seeds
1 - 2 tsp cumin seeds
750 g | 1 ¾ lbs spinach, washed

Method:
Heat the ghee in a pan and gently fry the onions for 10 minutes.

Add the chillies, ginger, coriander and cumin and cook for a further 5 minutes.

Add the spinach, cover and cook until it wilts. Stir well, cover and simmer for about 2 minutes. Season to taste.

Green lentils with lemon and chilli

Prep and cook time: 50 minutes
Cannot be frozen
Serves: 4

Ingredients:
175 g | 1 cup puy lentils, washed
3 tbsp fresh coriander|cilantro leaves
1 lemon, skinned, de-seeded
and chopped
3 tbsp olive oil
1 tsp brown mustard seeds
2 red chilli peppers, seeds removed,
cut into strips
2 garlic cloves, crushed

Method:

In 600 ml / 1 pint water, bring the lentils to a boil then allow to cook on a medium heat for 40 minutes with a lid on until the lentils are very soft. If necessary add a little more water.

Add the salt and coriander/cilantro, remove from the heat and add the lemon.

Heat the olive oil in a skillet, add the mustard seeds and allow them to pop. Add the chillies and the garlic and fry lightly. Add the contents of the skillet to the lentils, season and serve.

Green bean salad

Prep and cook time: 30 minutes
Cannot be frozen
Serves: 4

Ingredients:
2 tbsp coconut oil
1/2 tsp mustard seeds
1 small onion, finely chopped
1 garlic clove, finely chopped
2 red chilli peppers, halved lengthways
6 curry leaves
600 g | 4 cups green|string beans,
cut into small pieces
3 tbsp lemon juice
60 g | 3/4 cup coconut, grated

Method:
Heat the coconut oil in a skillet. Add the mustard seeds and fry, stirring continuously, until they begin to pop.

Add the onion, garlic, chilli and curry leaves and fry for a further 5 minutes, stirring continuously. Remove from the heat and let cool.

Cook the beans in boiling water for 2 minutes. Drain and quench in cold water.

Add the beans and the lemon juice to the mixture and allow to steep for a few minutes. Finally season to taste and serve in bowls garnished with the grated coconut.

Potatoes with cumin and coriander

Prep and cook time: 1 hour
Cannot be frozen
Serves: 4

Ingredients:
800 g | 6 cups potatoes
6 tbsp olive oil
1 tsp cumin seeds
4 cm | 1 ½" piece fresh ginger, peeled and chopped
½ tsp Cayenne pepper
3 tbsp fresh coriander|cilantro, finely chopped

Method:

Cook the potatoes in their skins in salt water for 25 minutes. Drain, let cool and then peel and dice.

Heat the oil in a non-stick skillet. Add the cumin seeds and fry on a medium heat for 5 minutes.

Add the potatoes and season with ginger, ground cumin, salt, Cayenne pepper and ground black pepper. Fry for a further 3-5 minutes turning often.

Remove the skillet from the heat. Stir in the coriander/cilantro and serve immediately.

meat
& fish.

Tandoori duck

Prep and cook time: 1 hour Marinate: 6 hours
Cannot be frozen
Serves: 4

Ingredients:
4 duck breast, skinned
200 g | ¾ cup yoghurt
1 tbsp apple vinegar
2 tbsp sesame oil
4 garlic cloves, crushed
2 cm | 1 ¼" piece fresh ginger,
peeled and chopped
2 tsp ground coriander
1 tsp cumin
1 tsp ground chilli powder
1 tsp turmeric

To serve:
1 cucumber, halved lengthways and
cut into 10 cm | 4" long strips
80 g | ½ cup pickled ginger, drained
1 lemon, sliced lengthways

Method:

Mix the yoghurt, vinegar and sesame oil. Stir in the garlic, ginger, coriander, cumin, chilli, turmeric and some pepper. Brush the meat with the marinade, cover and chill for at least 6 hours. Reserve excess marinade.

Heat the oven to 200°C (180°C fan) 400°F, gas 6.

Place the marinated duck in an oven proof dish covered with tin foil and cook in the middle of the hot oven for 20-25 minutes. Brush occasionally with the remaining marinade.

Serve the tandoori duck on plates with the cucumber, ginger and lemon slices.

Braised beef on banana leaves

Prep and cook time: 1 hour 50 minutes
Can be frozen
Serves: 4

Ingredients:
2 tsp cumin seeds
2 dried chilli peppers
1 tsp black peppercorns
4 cardamom pods
1 tsp ground cinnamon
1 tsp black mustard seeds
1 tsp fenugreek seeds
800 g | 5 cups stewing beef, diced
3 tbsp ghee
4 onions, chopped
3 garlic cloves, crushed
1 tsp fresh ginger, peeled
and chopped
1 tsp turmeric
2 tsp brown sugar
3 tbsp lemon juice
1 bay leaf
25 g | 1 cup coriander|cilantro,
roughly chopped
1 banana leaf, 30 cm | 12" long,
washed, dried and cut into wide strips

Method:
Grind the cumin seeds, chilli peppers, peppercorns, cardamom, cinnamon, mustard and fenugreek seeds in a blender.

Place the meat in a bowl and stir in the ground spices.

Heat 1 tbsp ghee in a skillet and fry the onions, garlic, ginger and turmeric on a medium heat for 2-3 minutes. Then puree in a blender along with the sugar.

Heat 2 tbsp ghee in the skillet and fry the meat on a medium heat. Season with salt and remove from the skillet.

Quench the meat juices with 400 ml / 1 ¾ cups water. Stir in the pureed onion mixture and the lemon juice and bring to a boil.

Place the fried meat back in the skillet along with the bay leaf and cook on a low heat for 1 hour or until the meat is tender.

Stir the coriander/cilantro in with the meat just before serving and season with salt and pepper.

To serve, place the banana leaves on the plate and arrange the meat on top. Serve with chapatis or Basmati rice.

Salmon fillet with peppers, raisins and zucchini

Prep and cook time: 40 minutes
Cannot be frozen
Serves: 4

Ingredients:
4 tbsp olive oil
2 onions, finely chopped
**2 red chilli peppers, seeds removed,
finely chopped**
1 tsp garam masala
$\frac{1}{2}$ tsp ground cumin
**2 medium courgettes|zucchinis,
sliced thinly**
**2 large green bell peppers, seeds
removed, cut into strips**
**4 tbsp raisins, soaked in a
little warm water**
300 ml | 1 $\frac{1}{4}$ cups vegetable stock
1 pinch Cayenne pepper
**800 g | 2 lbs salmon fillet, cut into
4 pieces**

Method:

Heat the oven to 180°C (160°C fan) 375°F, gas 5.

Heat the oil in a wide, ovenproof skillet or pan and cook the onion, chilli, garam masala and cumin until the onion is soft.

Add the courgettes/zucchinis and bell peppers and fry for about 2 minutes, stirring.

Add the drained raisins and the stock. Season with salt, pepper and Cayenne pepper and simmer for 5 minutes.

Place the salmon on the vegetables, spoon a little liquid over, cover and cook in the oven for 8-10 minutes.

Serve with saffron rice.

Chicken tikka

Prep and cook time: 40 minutes Marinade: 4 hours
Cannot be frozen
Serves: 4

Ingredients:
2 garlic cloves, crushed
1 tsp fresh ginger, peeled and grated
4 tbsp sesame oil
4 tbsp lime juice
2 tbsp yoghurt
$\frac{1}{2}$ tbsp tomato puree
$\frac{1}{2}$ tsp ground cardamom
1 tsp ground coriander
1 tsp ground cumin
$\frac{1}{2}$ tsp turmeric
1 tsp chilli powder
1 pinch ground cloves
4 chicken breasts, skinned and
cut into 1 cm strips

To garnish:
4 lime slices

Method:

Mix the garlic, ginger, sesame oil, lime juice, yoghurt and tomato puree. Stir in the cardamom, coriander, cumin, turmeric, chilli and cloves.

Add the chicken, cover and marinade in the refrigerator for at least 4 hours.

Remove the chicken from the marinade and grill for 3 minutes until the meat is just brown. Turn and grill for a further 3-5 minutes.

Season with salt and serve with the lime slices.

Tandoori fish masala

Prep and cook time: 35 minutes Marinate: 2 hours
Cannot be frozen
Serves: 4

Ingredients:
600 g | 1 ¼ lbs white fish filets,
cut into large pieces
2 tbsp lemon juice
2 tbsp melted ghee
400 g | 1 ⅔ cups yoghurt
3 tbsp vinegar
1 large onion, finely grated
4 garlic cloves, crushed
½ tsp fresh ginger, grated
1 tsp turmeric
1 pinch salt
1 pinch ground coriander
1 pinch garam masala
1 pinch chilli powder

To garnish:
½ red chilli pepper, seeds removed,
cut into rings
1 tbsp shallot, cut into rings
1 tbsp lime zest

Method:

Rub the fish with salt and lemon juice and place in a flat dish greased with ghee.

To make the marinade, mix all the ingredients with 1-2 tbsp water and pour over the fish. Cover and marinate in the refrigerator for about 2 hours, turning occasionally.

Heat the oven to 180°C (160°C fan) 375°F, gas 5.

Bake the fish for 15-20 minutes. If necessary add a little more water during cooking so the dish doesn't dry out.

Place the dish under a broiler / grill for a few minutes until the fish has browned slightly.

Serve in individual bowls with the chilli, shallot and lime zest sprinkled on top.

Duck with papaya chutney

Prep and cook time: 45 minutes
Cannot be frozen
Serves: 4

Ingredients:
2 duck breasts
$\frac{1}{2}$ tsp cumin seeds
1 tsp ground turmeric
1 pinch ground cloves
1/2 tsp ground coriander
3 cm | 1 $\frac{1}{4}$" piece fresh ginger,
peeled and chopped
$\frac{1}{2}$ red chilli pepper, seeds removed,
cut into fine strips
4 tbsp desiccated coconut
2 onions, chopped
1 papaya, seeds removed and
the flesh cut into pieces
1 orange, juiced and zest finely grated
1 orange, peeled and segmented,
pith removed
2 tbsp lime juice

To garnish:
8 slices coconut (optional)

Method:

Remove the duck skin from the meat and fry on a low heat for 3-4 minutes until all the fat has cooked out.

Cut the duck meat into bite-size pieces and place in a bowl with the cumin, turmeric, cloves and coriander. Remove the duck skin from the pot and discard.

Place the seasoned meat in the duck fat along with the ginger and chilli, fry on a medium heat for 4 minutes and season with a little salt.

Add the desiccated coconut. Fry for a further 3 minutes. Remove the meat and keep warm.

To make the chutney, quench the fat and meat juice with the orange juice and 100 ml / 7 tbsp water. Add the onion, cook gently for 5 minutes, then add the papaya, orange fillets and the lime juice. Bring to a boil and season with salt.

Serve the duck on plates with the papaya chutney and garnish with the orange zest and the coconut slices.

Chicken korma

Prep and cook time: 1 hour Marinate: 4 hours
Can be frozen
Serves: 4

Ingredients:
8 strands saffron
200 g | ³/₄ cup yoghurt
3 chicken breasts, skinned and cut into bite-size pieces
2 onions, finely chopped
3 garlic cloves, finely chopped
1 tsp fresh ginger, peeled and grated
2 red chilli peppers, cut into rings
50 g | ¹/₃ cup ground almonds
2 tbsp ghee
1 pinch ground cardamom
¹/₂ tsp ground cinnamon
1 ¹/₂ tsp ground cumin
1 ¹/₂ tsp ground coriander
1-2 lime leaves
2 curry leaves
400 ml | 1 ³/₄ cups coconut milk
2 tbsp chopped almonds

To garnish:
¹/₂ celery stalk, finely chopped

Method:
Dissolve the saffron in 1 tbsp hot water, mix with the yoghurt, add the chicken and marinate for 4 hours.

Mix the onions, garlic, ginger, chillies and ground almonds and set aside.

Heat the ghee in a pan and gently fry the cardamom, cinnamon, cumin and coriander. Then add the spice mixture from step 2 along with the lime and curry leaves and, stirring continuously, fry for 2-3 minutes

Add the coconut milk and the chicken, including the marinade, and cook very gently for 45 minutes.
Season with salt and sugar and stir in the chopped almonds.

Serve in bowls and garnish with the chopped celery.

Lamb in a cream sauce with cashew nuts

Prep and cook time: 1 hour 20 minutes
Can be frozen
Serves: 4

Ingredients:
800 g | 2 lbs lamb, from the leg,
cut into strips
3 tbsp vegetable oil
3 onions, chopped
2 garlic cloves, chopped
3 cardamom pods, slightly crushed
2 cloves
½ stick cinnamon
6 saffron threads
1 tsp ground coriander
1 tsp ground cumin
Cayenne pepper
3 tbsp lime juice
125 ml | ½ cup beef stock
50 g | ⅓ cup cashew nuts
100 ml | 7 tbsp cream

To garnish:
4 sprigs fresh coriander|cilantro

Method:
Heat the oil in a pan and fry the lamb on a high heat for
4 minutes, stirring continuously. Season with salt and
remove from the pan.

Add the onions and garlic to the pan and cook on a medium
heat. Add the cardamom pods, cloves, cinnamon stick, saffron,
ground coriander, cumin and Cayenne pepper and cook
for 2 minutes. Add the lime juice and stock and bring
to the boil.

Return the meat to the pan, add the cashew nuts, reduce the
heat and cook for 20 minutes with a lid on. Stir in the cream
and cook very gently for a further 30 minutes with the lid on
until the meat is tender. Season and serve garnished
with coriander/cilantro.

Sea bass steaks with Indian spices

Prep and cook time: 45 minutes
Cannot be frozen
Serves: 4

Ingredients:
2 tbsp ghee
2 onions, chopped
1 tsp turmeric
1 tbsp garam masala
1 tbsp red curry paste
2 tomatoes, roughly chopped
3 tbsp lime juice
50 ml | 10 tsp coconut milk
200 ml | 7/8 cup vegetable stock
4 sea bass steaks
8 sprigs coriander|cilantro, chopped

Method:

Heat the ghee in a deep skillet and fry the onions on a medium heat for 3-4 minutes.

Add the turmeric, garam masala, red curry paste and tomatoes and fry together for 1 minute. Stir in the lime juice, coconut milk and stock. Simmer for 5-8 minutes with a lid on.

Add the fish to the sauce and cook on a low heat for 7-10 minutes. The fish is cooked when the flesh comes away from the bone.

Just before serving stir the coriander/cilantro into the sauce. Season with salt and lime juice.

Butter chicken

Prep and cook time: 40 minutes Marinating time: 3 hours
Can be frozen
Serves: 4

Ingredients:
150 g yoghurt
3 tbsp finely ground almonds
2-3 tsp garam masala
1 good pinch Indian five-spice powder
1 good pinch cinnamon
1 good pinch ground cardamom
1 tsp ground ginger
2 cloves garlic, crushed
400 g | 1 ¾ cups canned tomatoes, chopped
1 tsp salt
4 medium chicken breasts, skinned and chopped into bite-sized chunks
3 tbsp ghee
4 onions, chopped
200 ml | ⅞ cup coconut milk
vegetable stock, as necessary
150 g | ½ lb spinach, washed

Method:
Mix the yoghurt, ground almonds, garam masala, five-spice mixture, cinnamon, cardamom, ginger, garlic, tomatoes and salt.

Put the chicken into a large bowl and pour the yoghurt sauce over them. Mix and leave to stand in a cool place for at least 3 hours (preferably overnight).

Heat the ghee in a deep skillet, add the onions and cook for 5 minutes.

Add the chicken and yoghurt mixture and cook for 10 minutes. Stir in the coconut milk and a little vegetable stock if the sauce is too thick. Bring to the boil over a low heat, stir in the spinach and cook very gently for 5 minutes.

Season to taste and serve.

Indian meat balls with a tomato and orange sauce

Prep and cook time: 45 minutes
Cannot be frozen
Serves: 4

Ingredients:
2 slices stale bread, crusts cut off
1 onion, finely chopped
2 garlic cloves, finely chopped
1 red chilli pepper, seeds removed, finely chopped
300 g | 1 ¼ cups ground lamb
300 g | 1 ¼ cups ground pork
2 sprigs mint, finely chopped
1 tsp ground turmeric
½ tsp ground coriander
½ tsp ground cumin
1 medium egg
½ tbsp yoghurt
200 g | 1 ⅛ cup Basmati rice
5 tbsp vegetable oil
1 can chopped tomatoes
20 g | ⅛ cup raisins
1 orange, juiced, zest finely grated
250 ml | 1 cup vegetable stock
poppadoms, to serve (optional)

To garnish:
2 sprigs mint

Method:
Place the bread in a bowl and cover with water.

Mix half the onion, garlic and chilli with the ground meat. Add the chopped mint, turmeric, coriander and cumin.

Wring out the bread and mix in with the meat along with the egg and yoghurt. Season well with salt and ground black pepper.

Bring a pan of salt water to the boil and cook the rice for 15 minutes or until al dente.

Heat 1 tbsp vegetable oil in a skillet. Fry the remaining onion, garlic and chilli for 3 minutes. Add the tinned tomatoes, raisins, orange zest and juice, and the vegetable stock. Season with salt and pepper and simmer for 5 minutes on a low heat. Keep warm.

With damp hands shape the meat into balls. Heat 4 tbsp vegetable oil in a large skillet and fry the meatballs on a medium heat for 10-12 minutes, turning as they cook. Add the cooked meatballs to the tomato-orange sauce and let the flavours steep for 5-10 minutes.

Serve on rice and with poppdums. Garnish with mint leaves.

Indian-style mince with potatoes and peas

Prep and cook time: 50 minutes
Can be frozen
Serves: 4

Ingredients:
3 tbsp ghee
600 g | 2 ½ cups ground meat,
pork or beef
2 onions, chopped
2 garlic cloves, chopped
2 chilli peppers, cut into rings
1 tsp fresh ginger, peeled
and finely chopped
1 tsp cumin seeds
1 tsp garam masala
½ tsp turmeric
250 ml | 1 cup beef stock
300 g | 2 cups baking potatoes, diced
1 tbsp paprika
150 g | 1 cup frozen peas
pinch Cayenne pepper

Method:
Heat the ghee in a skillet and gently fry the meat until lightly browned.

Add the onions, garlic, chilli, ginger, cumin, garam masala and turmeric and cook on a medium heat for 2 minutes.

Add the stock, potatoes and the paprika. Cook on a low heat for 20 minutes, stirring occasionally.

Stir in the peas and simmer for a further 10 minutes. Season with salt and Cayenne pepper and serve with naan bread.

Goa-style fish curry

Prep and cook time: 45 minutes
Cannot be frozen
Serves: 4

Ingredients:
1 lime, juiced
1 tsp fresh ginger, peeled and grated
½ tsp black mustard seeds
1 tbsp sesame seeds
1 tsp coriander seeds
2 tbsp sesame oil
600 g | 1 ½ lbs white fish fillets,
cut into large pieces
1 white onion, chopped
½ tsp ground turmeric
250 ml | 1 cup coconut milk
4 tomatoes, seeds removed, diced
200 g | 1 ⅛ cup Basmati rice
6 sprigs fresh coriander|cilantro
4 to garnish, 2 finely chopped

Method:
Bring a pan of water to the boil and add the rice.
Cook for 20 minutes.

Meanwhile, mix the lime juice with the ginger and mustard, sesame and coriander seeds. Add the fish and marinate for at least 15 minutes.

Heat the sesame oil in a large skillet. Remove the fish from the marinade, season with salt and fry on a medium heat for 5 minutes, turning carefully just once.

Remove the fish and set aside.

Fry the onions in the skillet and sprinkle with turmeric.
Add the remaining marinade and add the coconut milk.
Add the tomatoes and bring to the boil.

Place the fish in the sauce and heat for 2 minutes.
Season to taste.

Serve the fish curry on the rice, sprinkle with the chopped coriander/cilantro and garnish with the remaining sprigs.

Chicken tikka masala

Prep and cook time: 1 hour 25 minutes Marinade: 6 hours
Can be frozen
Serves: 4

Ingredients:
1 oven-ready chicken,
cut into 6-8 pieces
1 lemon

For the marinade:
2 tsp freshly grated ginger
2 cloves garlic, crushed
500 g | 18 oz | 2 cups yoghurt
2 tbsp vegetable oil
2 tbsp paprika
½ tsp ground cumin
½ tsp black pepper
½ tsp chilli powder
½ tsp turmeric
1 tbsp coriander|cilantro
leaves, chopped
300 g | 11 oz | 1 ½ cups rice

Method:
Score the surface of the chicken pieces to a depth of
½ cm / ¼" and put into a shallow dish. Sprinkle with pepper,
salt and the juice of a lemon. Let stand for
about 30 minutes.

Mix the garlic and ginger plus all the dried spices for the
marinade with the yoghurt. Coat the chicken pieces
generously with the marinade and seal the dish with
aluminium foil.

Marinate the chicken in the refrigerator for 8 hours or overnight.

Preheat the oven to 180°C (160°fan) 350°F, gas 5. Line a
cookie sheet with aluminium foil and put the chicken pieces
on the sheet. Cook in oven for 35-40 minutes, brushing
frequently with marinade (using about ¼), and adding a
little water if necessary.

Steam the rice according to the package instructions.

Heat the remaining marinade and add the chicken pieces.
Heat very gently for 5 minutes, then sprinkle with coriander/
cilantro and serve with rice.

Monkfish in a spicy tomato sauce

Prep and cook time: 25 minutes
Cannot be frozen
Serves: 4

Ingredients:
2 tbsp ghee
3 red onions, finely chopped
1 tsp fresh ginger, peeled
and finely chopped
2 garlic cloves, finely chopped
2 tbsp tomato puree
1 tsp ground coriander
½ tsp ground fennel seeds
½ tsp ground cumin
1 tsp chilli powder
1 tsp turmeric
1 tbsp brown sugar
3 tbsp lemon juice
600 g | 1 ½ lbs monkfish fillet,
cut into large pieces
8 sprigs coriander|cilantro,
roughly chopped

Method:

Heat the ghee in a pan and fry the onions, ginger and garlic on a medium heat for 3 minutes, stirring continuously.

Add the tomato puree, ground coriander, fennel, cumin, chilli and turmeric and fry for another minute. Sprinkle with sugar and allow to caramelize.

Add 250 ml / 1 cup water and the lemon juice and bring to the boil.

Add the fish and cook on a medium/low heat for 6-8 minutes. Stir in the coriander/cilantro, season with salt, ground black pepper and lemon juice and serve with Basmati rice.

Lamb rogan josh

Prep and cook time: 1 hour 25 minutes
Can be frozen
Serves: 4-6

Ingredients:
1 tsp fresh grated ginger
6 garlic cloves, crushed
6 tbsp peanut oil
8 cardamom pods
3 cm | 1" stick cinnamon
2 bay leaves
800 g | 2 lbs lamb, off the bone,
cut into bite-size pieces
2 onions
2 tsp cumin seeds, crushed
2 tsp ground coriander
1 pinch Cayenne pepper,
more if desired
1 tbsp sweet paprika
1-2 tbsp tomato puree

Method:
Mix the ginger and garlic together.

Heat the oil in a large skillet and cook the cardamom, cinnamon and bay leaves. Add the meat and fry until browned, then remove it from the skillet.

Add the onions and the ginger-garlic mixture to the skillet and fry gently until onions are translucent. Stir in the cumin, coriander, Cayenne pepper, paprika and tomato puree and cook for a further 2 minutes.

Place the meat back in the skillet, add 300 ml / 1 ¼ cups of water, bring to a boil and simmer for 1 hour. Serve with rice.

Duck soup with mango

Prep and cook time: 1 hour 30 minutes
Can be frozen
Serves: 4

Ingredients:
4 duck legs
1 onion, chopped
100 g | ⅔ cup celeriac|celery root,
peeled and diced
1 carrot, diced
2 bay leaves
½ tsp peppercorns
4 cm | 1 ½" piece fresh ginger,
peeled and grated
2 garlic cloves, finely chopped
1 mango, peeled, 8 slices to garnish,
remainder finely chopped
2 spring onions|scallions, cut into rings
1 tsp curry powder

Method:
Put the duck legs in a pan with 1½ litres / 3 pints water and ½ tsp salt and bring to the boil.

Add the onion, celeriac/celery root, carrot, bay leaves and peppercorns to the pan. Simmer for 40-45 minutes, removing the scum as it rises to the surface.

Strain the broth into a bowl and let cool. As soon the fat has risen to the top, scoop it off with a ladle and reserve.

Let the cooked duck legs cool and remove the skin.
Cut the meat from the bone and chop into bite-size pieces.

Heat 2 tbsp reserved duck fat in a pan and gently fry the ginger and garlic with the chopped mango and the spring onions/scallions. Stir in the curry powder and slowly pour in the broth.

Simmer on a medium heat for 3 minutes. Add the meat and keep warm.

Season to taste and serve the soup.

Prawn curry

Prep and cook time: 35 minutes
Cannot be frozen
Serves: 4

Ingredients:
1 tsp Cayenne pepper
1/2 tsp turmeric
1 tbsp ground coriander
1 tsp ground cumin
2 tbsp lemon juice
3 tbsp peanut oil
1/2 tsp brown mustard seeds
1 onion, finely chopped
2 garlic cloves, crushed
400 ml | 1 2/3 cups coconut milk
500 g | 2 cups raw prawns|shrimps,
with tails, halved lengthways

Method:
In a bowl mix the Cayenne pepper, turmeric, coriander, cumin, lemon juice, 1/2 tsp salt and 100 ml / 7 tbsp water.

Heat the peanut oil in a skillet and add the mustard seeds. As soon as they begin to pop, add the onion and garlic and fry the mixture until golden brown.

Add the spice mixture from step 1 and simmer for 5 minutes.

Stir in the coconut milk and bring to a boil. Add the prawns|shrimps and simmer for 2-3 minutes or until they are cooked. Season with salt, ground black pepper and lemon juice.

Serve with rice or chapatis.

Chicken curry with saffron rice

Prep and cook time: 45 minutes
Can be frozen
Serves: 4

Ingredients:
200 g | 1 ⅛ cup Basmati rice
1 pinch ground saffron
1 lime, one half juiced, one half sliced
to garnish
4 chicken breasts, skinned and cut into
bite-size pieces
1 tbsp curry powder
½ tsp sambal ulek or hot chilli paste
2 tbsp ghee
2 onions, chopped
350 ml | 1 ½ cups coconut milk
100 ml | 7 tbsp chicken stock
4 tomatoes, diced
4 sprigs fresh coriander|cilantro

Method:
Put the rice in 300 ml salt water and bring to a boil. Stir in the saffron and then simmer on the lowest heat for 18-20 minutes. Keep warm.

Drizzle the lime juice over the chicken and stir in the curry powder and the sambal ulek.

Heat the ghee in a large skillet and fry the chicken on a high heat for 3 minutes. Season with salt and ground black pepper and remove from the skillet.

Add the onions to the skillet and fry gently on a medium/low heat for 3-4 minutes. Stir in the coconut milk and the stock. Bring to a boil, add the chicken and simmer on a low heat for 8 minutes.

Add the tomatoes and warm gently in the sauce.
Season to taste.

Arrange the curry on plate and garnish with the coriander/cilantro and lime slices. Serve with the saffron rice.

Bhuna ghost

Prep and cook time: 1 hour 45 minutes Marinate: 30 minutes
Can be frozen
Serves: 4

Ingredients:

1 tsp fresh ginger, peeled and chopped
1 chilli pepper, seeds
removed, chopped
1 tbsp garam masala
800 g | 2 lbs lean lamb,
cut into large chunks
6 tbsp vegetable oil
4 onions, diced
2 garlic cloves, sliced
$\frac{1}{2}$ tsp ground cumin
1 tsp paprika
2 tbsp tomato puree
3 tomatoes, diced
8 sprigs fresh coriander|cilantro,
finely chopped
4 tbsp yoghurt

Method:

Mix half the ginger and chilli pepper with the garam masala and rub into the lamb chunks. Marinate at room temperature for at least 30 minutes.

Heat 2 tbsp oil in a large pan and fry half the onion and garlic with the remaining ginger and chilli pepper on a medium/low heat. Season with cumin, salt, ground black pepper and paprika. Remove from the pan and set aside.

Heat 4 tbsp oil in the pan and fry the lamb on a medium heat for 5 minutes. Season with salt, remove from the pan and set aside.

Stir the tomato puree into the meat juices, add the remaining onion and garlic and cook gently for 1 minute. Add 750 ml / 1.5 pints water, mix well with a wooden spoon and bring to a boil.

Place the lamb back in the pan, reduce the heat and cook very gently, stirring occasionally, for one hour or until the meat is tender.

Season the curry with salt and ground black pepper and divide between 4 bowls.

Garnish with the coriander/cilantro, diced tomatoes, yoghurt and spicy onions from step 2.

Sea bass with peanut sauce and spicy onions

Prep and cook time: 50 minutes
Cannot be frozen
Serves: 4

Ingredients:
2 medium sweet potatoes, scrubbed
3 onions, finely chopped
5 tbsp vegetable oil
5 cm | 2" piece fresh ginger, peeled and finely chopped
2 garlic cloves, finely chopped
2 tbsp peanut butter, smooth
250 ml | 1 cup coconut milk
5 tbsp lime juice
1 tsp chilli powder
1 tsp turmeric
1 tsp ground coriander
1 tsp ground cumin
3 tsp desiccated coconut
600 g | 1 ½ lbs sea bass, with skin

Method:

Put the sweet potatoes into a pan of water, bring to the boil and cook for 15-20 minutes or until tender.

To make the peanut sauce, heat 1 tbsp oil in a small pan. Fry a third of the onions until translucent then add the ginger and garlic. Stir in the peanut butter and add the coconut milk.

Simmer for 5 minutes until the sauce becomes thick. Season with lime juice, salt and pepper and keep warm.

To make the spicy onions, heat 2 tbsp oil in a skillet and fry the remaining onions on a low heat for 4 minutes. Add the chilli powder, turmeric, coriander and cumin and stir in the desiccated coconut. Cook for a further 2 minutes, stirring continuously. Season and remove from the skillet.

Cut the sweet potatoes in half lengthwise and sprinkle with 1 tsp salt, 1 tbsp oil and 1 tbsp lime juice. Place the potatoes on a cookie sheet or a rack and grill for 5 minutes until slightly crispy.

Drizzle the fish with 2 tbsp lime juice. Heat 1 tbsp oil in the skillet and fry the fish on a medium heat for 6 minutes, turning once.

Put one half sweet potato and some peanut sauce on each plate. Place the fish on top and sprinkle with the spicy onions.

Spicy pork with tomatoes and chapatis

Prep and cook time: 1 hour
Can be frozen
Serves: 4

Ingredients:
For the chapatis:
¹/₂ **tsp salt**
100 g | 1 cup plain|all purpose flour, or wholegrain flour
1 tbsp ghee

For the spicy pork:
600 g | 1 ¹/₂ lbs pork shoulder, diced
2 garlic cloves, chopped
1 tsp ginger, chopped
1 pinch ground cinnamon
1 pinch ground cardamom
1 pinch ground coriander
1 pinch turmeric
2 tbsp ghee
1 onion, chopped
¹/₂ **tbsp brown sugar**
3 tbsp lemon juice
250 ml | 1 cups vegetable stock
4 tomatoes, quartered
4 sprigs parsley, chopped

To garnish:
4 sprigs parsley, whole

Method:
To make the chapatis, dissolve the salt in 60 ml / ¹/₄ cup water. Stir in the flour and the ghee and knead into a soft dough. Shape the dough into a ball, cover and allow to rest for 30 minutes.

Mix the meat with the garlic and ginger and stir in the cinnamon, cardamom, coriander and turmeric.

Heat the ghee in a skillet and fry the meat for 4 minutes on a high heat. Season with salt and ground black pepper and remove.

Fry the onion in the skillet on a low heat for 4 minutes. Return the meat back to the skillet, sprinkle with sugar and allow to caramelize, stirring frequently.

Add the lemon juice and vegetable stock. Simmer for 3-5 minutes until the liquid has reduced to about half. Keep warm.

Divide the chapati dough into 4 portions and roll out on a floured work surface. Cook in a hot, dry skillet on both sides until brown.

Mix the tomatoes and parsley into the spicy pork, season with salt and pepper and serve with the chapatis.

Safed maas – lamb curry in a spicy cream sauce

Prep and cook time: 1 hour 30 minutes
Can be frozen
Serves: 4

Ingredients:
800 g | 2 lbs boned lean lamb, diced
1 tsp fresh grated ginger
1 tsp cardamom pods, slightly crushed
1 tsp garam masala
½ tsp ground cloves
1 dried chilli pepper
2 tbsp ghee
2 tbsp plain|all purpose flour
2 onions, chopped
400 ml | 1 ¾ cups meat stock
50 ml | 10 tsp cream
200 g | ¾ cup yoghurt

Method:
Mix the lamb with the ginger, cardamom pods, garam masala, ground cloves and dried chilli pepper. Allow to marinade for at least 15 minutes.

Heat the ghee in a large skillet. Mix the marinated meat with the flour and fry in the hot fat on a medium heat.
Season with salt.

Add the onions and sweat for 2 minutes. Pour on the stock and, stirring continuously, bring to the boil. Allow the curry to cook on a low heat, stirring occasionally, for 30 minutes with a lid on.

Add the cream and cook for a further 30 minutes with a lid on. Just before serving stir in the yoghurt and season with salt.

Spicy prawns

Prep and cook time: 25 minutes
Cannot be frozen
Serves: 4

Ingredients:
200 g | 1 ⅛ cup Basmati rice
2 tbsp ghee
600 g | 2 ¼ cups raw prawns|shrimps, in their shells
2 garlic cloves, sliced
1 red chilli pepper, seeds removed, finely sliced
8 saffron threads
1 tsp turmeric
1 tsp garam masala
3 tbsp lemon juice
250 ml | 1 cup coconut milk
1 red bell pepper, sliced

To garnish:
4 lemon slices

Method:
Bring a pan of salt water to the boil and cook the rice for 15 minutes.

Heat the ghee in a skillet and fry the prawns/shrimps on a high heat for 2 minutes. Add the garlic, chilli, saffron threads, turmeric and garam masala. Add the lemon juice and coconut milk.

Add the bell pepper and simmer for 5 minutes with a lid on. Season with salt, ground black pepper and lemon juice.

Serve the prawns/shrimps with rice and garnish with lemon slices.

Fish madras

Prep and cook time: 20 minutes
Cannot be frozen
Serves: 4

Ingredients:
4 onions
200 ml | ⅞ cup vegetable stock,
more if required
600 g | 1 ½ lbs white fish fillets
1 tbsp rice starch
2 - 3 tbsp oil
3 - 4 tbsp madras curry paste

Method:
Puree the onion with a little of the stock in a blender.

Dust the fish with the rice starch. Heat the oil in a skillet and fry the fish quickly on both sides. Remove from the skillet.

Add the curry paste, pureed onions and the remaining stock to the skillet. Heat, stirring continuously, then add the fish and allow to steep on a gentle heat for 5-8 minutes. If necessary add a little more stock or water. Serve with rice.

Jalfrezi

Prep and cook time: 20 minutes
Can be frozen
Serves: 4

Ingredients:
3 tbsp oil
¼ tsp black mustard seeds
¼ tsp cumin seeds
3 onions, finely sliced
3 green chilli peppers, seeds removed,
cut into thin strips
500 g | 1 ¼ lbs lamb or duck,
cut into thin strips
¼ tsp ground coriander
¼ tsp turmeric
1 tbsp Worcester Sauce
3 tomatoes, peeled, seeds removed,
finely chopped

Method:
Heat the oil in a skillet and fry the mustard and cumin seeds for about 30 seconds until they begin to crackle. Add the onion and the chilli peppers and fry gently, stirring continuously.

Stir in the meat, ground spices, Worcester sauce and tomatoes. Season with salt and pepper and fry together on a medium heat for a further 3-5 minutes.

Serve with rice.

Hot and spicy sweet and sour prawn curry

Prep and cook time: 30 minutes
Cannot be frozen
Serves: 4

Ingredients:
1 tbsp ghee
1 tbsp garam masala
2 cloves garlic, finely chopped
100 ml | 7 tbsp fish stock
300 ml | 1 ¼ cups coconut milk
600 g | 2 ½ cups raw prawns|shrimps ,
shelled and cleaned
400 g | 2 cups beefsteak tomatoes,
skinned, deseeded and chopped
2 tbsp honey
2 tbsp vinegar
Cayenne pepper

To garnish:
1 tbsp fresh coriander|cilantro
leaves, chopped

Method:
Heat the ghee in a skillet and briefly sauté the garam masala.

Add the garlic, fry briefly then add the fish stock. Bring to the boil and add the coconut milk. Simmer over a low heat for about 2 minutes.

Add the prawns/shrimps , tomatoes, honey, vinegar, salt and Cayenne pepper to taste. Cover and cook very gently for 2-3 minutes, until the prawns/shrimps are cooked.

Serve sprinkled with coriander/cilantro.

Lamb vindaloo

Prep and cook time: 2 hours 15 minutes Marinate: 2 hours
Can be frozen
Serves: 4

Ingredients:

2 cloves, ground
2 cm | ¾ in cinnamon stick
½ tsp cardamom seeds
1 tsp cumin seeds
1 tsp coriander seeds
50 ml | 10 tsp malt vinegar
800 g | 2 lbs lamb, chopped
into bite-sized chunks
2 onions, diced
2 tbsp ghee
4 garlic cloves, chopped
1 tsp fresh ginger, peeled and grated
2 red chilli peppers, chopped
200 g | ⅞ cup canned
tomatoes, chopped
600 ml | 2 ½ cups chicken stock
1 tsp brown sugar
1 tsp peppercorns, crushed
2 tsp lime juice

To garnish:
parsley leaves

Method:

Finely grind the cloves, cinnamon, cardamom, cumin and coriander in a mortar. Add the vinegar and pour the mixture over the meat in a bowl. Mix well, cover and leave to marinade for about 2 hours.

Heat the ghee in a pan and gently brown the onions. Reduce the heat, add the garlic, ginger, chilli peppers and tomatoes and leave to braise for about 2 minutes.

Add the meat along with its marinade. Pour the stock into the pan, add the sugar and peppercorns, cover with a lid and braise for about 1 ½ - 2 hours over a low heat until the meat is tender. Add more water if necessary.

Season with salt and lime juice. Garnish with parsley leaves to serve.

vegetarian.

Tarka dhal

Prep and cook time: 1 hour
Can be frozen
Serves: 4

Ingredients:
75 g | ³/₈ cup red lentils
75 g | ³/₈ cup yellow mung beans
¹/₂ tsp turmeric
900 ml | 4 cups water
salt
3 tbsp groundnut oil
¹/₂ tsp cumin seeds
2 red chilli peppers, chopped
1 clove garlic, lightly crushed
and peeled

Method:

Wash and drain the lentils and mung beans. Put into a pan with the turmeric and water, bring to the boil, cover and simmer gently for 40 – 45 minutes. Season with salt.

Heat the oil in a skillet and fry the cumin, chillies and garlic until they begin to darken. Mix with the cooked beans and lentils and spoon onto plates.

Chickpea korma

Prep and cook time: 15 minutes
Can be frozen
Serves: 4

Ingredients:
250 g | 1 ¼ cups chickpeas|garbanzo beans
2 onions, finely chopped
3 garlic cloves, finely chopped
2 red chilli peppers, cut into rings
1 tsp fresh grated ginger
50 g | ⅓ cup ground almonds
2 tbsp ghee
1 pinch ground cardamom
½ tsp ground cinnamon
1 ½ tsp ground cumin
1 tsp ground coriander
400 g coconut milk
1 ½ tsp garam masala
150 g | ¾ cup cherry tomatoes, quartered

To garnish:
1 spring onion|scallion, diagonally sliced

Method:

Mix together the onions, garlic, chilli, ginger and almonds.

Melt the ghee in a pot and add the cardamom, cinnamon, cumin and coriander and fry gently together. Then add the onion-spice mixture prepared in step 1. Fry, stirring continuously, for 2-3 minutes.

Add the coconut milk and chickpeas/garbanzo beans and simmer uncovered for 45 minutes, stirring occasionally.

Stir the garam masala into the korma and season with salt. Add the tomatoes towards the end and allow to steep for 1-2 minutes.

Serve with rice and garnished with spring onion/scallion rings.

Cauliflower curry

Prep and cook time: 45 minutes
Can be frozen
Serves: 4

Ingredients:
250 g | 8 ¹/₃ cups spinach leaves
2 tbsp oil
500 g | 3 ¹/₅ cups baking
potatoes, diced
700 g | 7 cups cauliflower florets
2 garlic cloves, chopped
1 ¹/₂ small green chilli peppers,
seeds removed, finely chopped
2 tsp fresh root ginger, grated
3 tsp garam masala
200 g | 1 cup low-fat yoghurt
1 tsp flour
300 g | 1 ¹/₄ cups chickpeas|garbanzo
beans, well drained
3 tbsp lemon juice
paprika, hot

Method:

Drop the spinach leaves into boiling salt water.
Drain immediately and press out excess water.

Heat the oil in a high skillet. Fry the potatoes, stirring often,
for 10 minutes. Add the cauliflower. If necessary add
some hot water and cook for a further 10 minutes.

Add the garlic, chillies and ginger to the skillet and
fry quickly. Stir in the garam masala.

Mix the yoghurt and flour together to form a smooth paste
and add to the potatoes along with the chickpeas/garbanzo
beans. Simmer everything at a low heat for 10 minutes
and at the end stir in the spinach.

Season the curry with lemon juice, salt and ground black
pepper. Serve sprinkled with paprika.

Hard boiled eggs in moghlai sauce

Prep and cook time: 25 minutes
Cannot be frozen
Serves: 4

Ingredients:
1/2 tsp Cayenne pepper
1/2 tsp ground cumin
1/2 tsp garam masala
1/2 tsp ground coriander
1 tbsp lemon juice
2 tbsp peanut oil
1 onion, finely chopped
1 tsp fresh ginger, peeled and grated
1 tsp tomato puree
150 ml | 2/3 cup chicken stock
100 ml | 7 tbsp crème fraiche
100 ml | 7 tbsp cream
2 tbsp coriander|cilantro leaves,
finely chopped
8 hard boiled eggs, peeled
and halved lengthways

To garnish:
4 sprigs coriander|cilantro

Method:

Mix the Cayenne pepper, cumin, garam masala, ground coriander, lemon juice, salt and some pepper in 1 tbsp water.

Heat the oil in a large skillet and quickly fry the onions. Add the ginger and stir. Add the tomato puree and the spice mixture and quench with the stock.

Add the crème fraiche and cream and simmer for 5 minutes. Then add the coriander/cilantro and season.

Pour the sauce over the eggs and garnish with coriander/cilantro leaves. Serve with pitta bread.

Potato curry with mango and poppy seeds

Prep and cook time: 50 minutes
Cannot be frozen
Serves: 4

Ingredients:
2 tbsp ghee
1 onion, finely chopped
1 garlic clove, finely chopped
1 tsp fresh ginger, peeled and grated
1 tsp turmeric
1 pinch Cayenne pepper
700 g | 1 ¾ lbs potatoes, cut into
bite-size pieces
500 ml | 2 cups vegetable stock
200 g | ½ lb spinach, selected leaves
1 tsp ground cardamom
1 pinch ground cinnamon
1 pinch ground cloves
1 pinch garam masala
1 pinch ground cumin
1 small mango, finely sliced

To garnish:
1 tsp poppy seeds
1 red chilli pepper, seeds removed,
cut into long thin strips

Method:
Heat the ghee and quickly fry the onions, garlic and ginger. Stir in the turmeric and Cayenne pepper, add the potatoes and fry together.

Add the stock and cook for 15 minutes with a lid on. Then add the spinach and simmer for a further 5 minutes. Season with salt and ground black pepper.

Dry roast the cardamom, cinnamon, cloves, garam masala and cumin in a small skillet until the scents become noticeable.

Stir the spice mixture into the potato curry and season.

Arrange into small bowls with the mango. Garnish with poppy seeds and chilli.

Sindhi kadi – vegetable stew with tamarind and chilli

Prep and cook time: 45 minutes
Cannot be frozen
Serves: 4

Ingredients:
1/2 tsp fennel seeds
1/2 tsp cumin
1/2 tsp coriander seeds
5 tbsp ghee
1 tsp turmeric
800 g | 5 1/3 cups potatoes, diced
200 g | 2 cups okra pods,
halved lengthways
2 tbsp gram (chickpea) flour
4 tbsp tamarind pods
2 bananas, sliced

Method:
Grind the fennel seeds, cumin and coriander together in a mortar.

Heat the ghee and fry the ground seeds with the turmeric. Add the potatoes and the okra pods and dust with the gram flour.

Add 750 ml / 1 1/2 pints water and simmer for 15 minutes. Add the tamarind pods and the bananas and simmer for a further 5-10 minutes until thick. Season with salt and serve with either rice or bread.

Filled aubergines with Paneer cheese

Prep and cook time: 1 hour 15 minutes
Cannot be frozen
Serves: 4

Ingredients:
250 ml | 9 fl oz | 1 cup vegetable stock
250 g | 9 oz | 1 ½ cups couscous
4 aubergines|eggplants,
halved lengthways
2 tbsp ghee
2 onions, finely chopped
2 carrots, finely chopped
1 green bell pepper, finely chopped
8 button mushrooms, sliced
1 tbsp garam masala
100 g | 3 ½ oz | ²/₅ cup Paneer
cheese, crumbled

Method:
Heat the oven to 180°C (160°C fan) 375°F, gas 5.

Pour the boiling stock over the couscous and allow to
soak for approximately 5 minutes.

Hollow out the aubergine/eggplant halves leaving
2 cm around the edge. Chop the hollowed out flesh.

Heat the ghee and fry the onions, carrots, bell pepper,
mushrooms and aubergine/eggplant flesh. Season with
salt and garam masala and stir into the couscous.
Fill the aubergine/eggplant halves with this mixture.

Sprinkle the Paneer cheese over the aubergine/eggplant
halves and bake for 45 minutes in either an oven-proof dish or
on a roasting tray.

Tempeh – spicy soy bread

Prep and cook time: 40 minutes
Cannot be frozen
Serves: 4

Ingredients:
1 bunch spring onions|scallions,
sliced diagonally into thin rings
3 cloves garlic, crushed
450 g | 2 cups tempeh,
cut into 1 cm / ½ in slices
250 ml | 1 cups vegetable oil
1 tsp hot chilli sauce
2 tsp lump sugar
salt
6 tbsp sweet soy sauce

Method:

Heat the oil in a skillet and fry the tempeh slices until they are crunchy. Remove them from the pan.

Fry the spring onions/scallions and garlic at medium heat in the remaining oil until they are transparent.

Add chilli sauce, lump sugar and salt and cover with soy sauce. Cook for about 1 minute.

Put the tempeh into the pan and mix it carefully with the sauce. Serve either warm or cold.

Ayurvedic vegetable cake

Prep and cook time: 50 minutes
Cannot be frozen
Serves: 4

Ingredients:
For the base:
500 ml | 2 cups milk
250 g | 1 ½ cups instant polenta
1 tsp dried Provencal herbs
1 pinch turmeric
1 pinch garam masala
1 pinch amchur powder
(mango powder)
1 pinch sugar

For the topping:
1 medium courgette|zucchini,
thinly sliced
4-5 ripe tomatoes, sliced
125 g | ½ cup smoked tofu, diced
150 g | ⅔ cup tinned sweetcorn,
drained
1 chilli pepper, seeds removed, diced
2 carrots, grated
1 handful rocket|arugula
1 carrot, roughly grated

Plus:
1 tbsp ghee, for greasing

Method:
Heat the oven to 180°C (160°C fan) 375°F, gas 5.

To make the base, boil the milk in a pot and stir in the polenta, herbs, turmeric, garam masala, amchur powder and sugar. Set aside and allow to rest for 5-10 minutes. Then pour onto a cookie sheet greased with non-stick paper, smooth and cool.

Decoratively arrange the courgettes/zucchini, tomatoes, tofu and sweetcorn on the polenta base and sprinkle with the chilli. Bake for 15-20 minutes.

Arrange the carrot and rocket/arugula on 4 plates. Remove the cake from the oven, cut into pieces and serve with the salad.

Cauliflower dhal

Prep and cook time: 50 minutes
Cannot be frozen
Serves: 4

Ingredients:
3 tbsp ghee
1 tsp garam masala
2 onions, finely chopped
1 red chilli pepper, seeds removed,
finely chopped
2 bay leaves
1 tsp turmeric
1 tsp ground cumin
200 g | 1 cup red lentils, washed
600 g | 6 cups cauliflower florets
1 green bell pepper, seeds
removed, roughly chopped
4 tomatoes, peeled, finely chopped

To garnish:
3 sprigs fresh coriander|cilantro,
roughly chopped

Method:

Heat the ghee in a pot add the garam masala and fry the onions stirring continuously. Add the chilli, bay leaves, turmeric and cumin and fry together for 2 minutes.

Add the lentils, cauliflower, bell pepper and tomatoes.
Pour on with 750 ml / 3 cups water, bring to a boil and simmer for 25 minutes. If necessary add a little more water.

Season with salt, serve in bowls and garnish with the coriander|cilantro.

Chickpea dumplings in a spicy sauce

Prep and cook time: 1 hours 10 minutes
Cannot be frozen
Serves: 4

Ingredients:
250 g yoghurt
2-3 tbsp oil
1 tbsp cumin seeds
2 tbsp fresh ginger, peeled and grated
2 tbsp dried fenugreek
325 g |3 $^1/_5$ cups gram (chickpea) flour
1 pinch baking soda
(bicarbonate soda)

For the sauce:
2 - 3 tbsp ghee
2 cloves
1 cinnamon stick
2 bay leaves
1 tbsp curry powder
1 pinch asafoetida
1 tsp ground coriander
1-2 tsp chilli flakes

To garnish:
2 tbsp cilantro|coriander leaves, chopped
2 $^1/_2$ cm | 1" fresh ginger, finely sliced

Method:
Mix 1/3 of the yoghurt with the oil, $^1/_2$ tbsp cumin seeds, the grated ginger, fenugreek and 125 ml / 1 cup water.

Mix together the gram flour, baking soda and salt and knead into the yoghurt mixture. If necessary add some more flour or water. Knead until a firm dough is formed.

Shape the dough into long sausages each 2 cm / 1" diameter.

Cut the dough strands into pieces 2 cm / 1" long and then cook in a boiling salt water for 15-20 minutes

Drain and set aside, but keep the water.

For the sauce heat the ghee and roast the remaining cumin seeds, cloves, cinnamon stick and the bay leaves.

Add the curry powder and the asafoetida. Reduce the heat and stir in the coriander, remaining yoghurt and 375 ml / 13 fl oz of the left over water used for boiling.

Add the chilli flakes, season with salt and allow to cook. Lay the chickpea dumplings in the sauce.

Serve garnished with coriander/cilantro leaves and chopped ginger.

Ek handi nu dhal bhaat

Prep and cook time: 55 minutes
Cannot be frozen
Serves: 4

Ingredients:
4 tbsp ghee
2 green chilli peppers, cut into rings
1 onion, finely chopped
1 garlic clove, finely chopped
1/2 tsp cumin
3 cloves
1/2 tsp peppercorns
1 bay leaf
1 tsp fresh ginger, peeled and grated
400 g | 3 cups baking potatoes, halved
150 g | 3/4 cup red lentils
1/2 tsp Cayenne pepper
1/2 tsp garam masala
100 g | 1/3 cup canned tomatoes
2 tbsp coriander|cilantro
leaves, chopped

For the rice:
200 g | 1 1/8 cups Basmati rice
1/2 tsp turmeric

For the sauce:
2 tbsp ghee
2 garlic cloves, finely chopped
2 dried, red chilli peppers, halved
1 tsp fennel seeds
1 tsp turmeric
1/2 tsp cumin
200 ml | 7/8 cup coconut milk
1 tbsp coriander|cilantro
leaves, whole

Method:
Heat the ghee and fry the chilli, onion and garlic. Add the cumin, cloves, peppercorns, bay leaf and ginger then add 400 ml / 1 2/3 cups water.

Add the potatoes, lentils, Cayenne pepper, garam masala, tomatoes and coriander/cilantro and stew on a gentle heat for 25 minutes, covered, stirring occasionally. Season with salt.

Put the rice and turmeric together in a pot of 250 ml / 1 cup water. Bring to a boil and then simmer for 20 minutes, covered. If necessary add a little more water.

To make the curry sauce, heat the ghee and sweat the garlic and chilli. Add the fennel seeds, turmeric and cumin and fry together for 1 minute. Then quench with 100 ml / 1/2 cup water and the coconut milk and simmer for 10 minutes.

Add the coriander/cilantro leaves and season with salt. Serve the lentils and potatoes on the rice with the curry sauce on the side.

Creamy black bean soup

Prep and cook time: 40 minutes
Can be frozen
Serves: 4

Ingredients:
2 tbsp oil
1 large onion, chopped
2 cloves garlic, crushed
1 tsp root ginger, grated
1 tsp ground cumin
1/2 tsp ground turmeric
800 ml | 28 fl oz | 3 ½ cups
vegetable stock
1 sundried tomato, chopped
600 g | 21 oz canned black beans,
drained and rinsed
200 ml | 7 fl oz | ⁷/₈ cup single cream
3 tsp balsamic vinegar

To garnish:
4 tbsp natural yoghurt
Several sprigs of dill

Method:

Heat the oil in a large pan, add the onion and garlic and fry for a few minutes, to soften.

Add the ginger, cumin and turmeric and fry for 30 seconds. Then pour in the stock.

Add the tomato and the beans. Bring to the boil, season with salt and ground black pepper, then turn down the heat and simmer for 30 minutes.

Take out half of the beans, puree the soup, then put the beans back into the soup.

Stir in the cream, reheat the soup and season to taste with vinegar.

If the soup is too thick, stir in a little more vegetable stock or water.

Ladle into bowls, add a swirl of yoghurt to each and garnish with dill.

Vegetable curry with peppers and couscous

Prep and cook time: 35 minutes
Can be frozen
Serves: 4

Ingredients:
4 tbsp sunflower oil
1 tsp chilli powder
2 tsp turmeric
3 onions, sliced
4 red peppers, deseeded and
cut into strips
1 red chilli pepper, deseeded, washed
and cut into thin strips
500 g | 18 oz cooked potatoes, peeled
and quartered
4 cloves garlic, peeled and crushed
200 g | 7 oz can chickpeas|garbanzo
beans, drained
400 g | 14 oz can coconut milk
300 g | 11 oz | 1 ½ cups couscous
2 tbsp butter, melted

To garnish:
4 sprigs of mint

Method:
Heat the sunflower oil in a wok and fry 1 tsp chilli powder
and 2 tsp turmeric for 20 seconds.

Add the onions for 4 minutes, then add the peppers, chilli
and potatoes and fry, stirring constantly, for 5 minutes.

Crush in the garlic and mix in the chickpeas/garbanzo beans.
Pour in the coconut milk.

Cover and cook for about 20 minutes. Season to taste with salt
and ground pepper.

Meanwhile put the couscous into a bowl and cover with
300 ml / 10 fl oz / 1 ¼ cups boiling water, season and leave
to stand for 10 minutes.

Pour on the melted butter; stir through the couscous with a fork.

Serve the vegetable curry in bowls with the couscous and
garnished with mint leaves.

Vegetable biryani

Prep and cook time: 1 hour 45 minutes
Cannot be frozen
Serves: 6-8

Ingredients:
4 tbsp ghee
3 onions, chopped
400 g | 1 ¾ cups Basmati rice
¼ tsp ground cinnamon
½ tsp ground turmeric
¼ tsp ground cardamom
½ tsp ground cumin
4 cm | 1 ½" fresh ginger,
peeled and grated
3 cloves
2 bay leaves
300 g | 3 cups cauliflower florets
300 g | 2 cups potatoes, peeled
and roughly diced
200 g | 1 ¼ cups peas, frozen
2 tomatoes, quartered
3 tbsp yoghurt
¼ tsp chilli powder
2 tbsp flaked|slivered almonds
2 tbsp raisins

To garnish:
4 eggs, hard-boiled, shelled
and quartered
1 lime, cut into wedges

Method:
Soak a Römertopf (unglazed clay pot) in cold water.

Heat 2 tbsp ghee in a pan and sweat 1 onion until translucent. Stir in the rice and cook for about 3 minutes.
Add 250 ml / 1 cup water, bring to the boil and cook very gently over a very low heat for 5 minutes. The rice should be only half-cooked. Remove from the heat and leave to steam dry.

Heat the rest of the ghee in a pan and add all the ground spices with the grated ginger, cloves and bay leaves. Fry for a minute or so, then add the rest of the onions, the cauliflower and the potatoes. Stir well and cook for 3 minutes.

Add the peas and tomatoes and stir in the yoghurt and 250 ml / 1 cup water. Season with chilli powder, salt and ground black pepper, cover and simmer for a further 4 minutes.

Spread half the rice on the base of the soaked Römertopf. Scatter with the flaked/slivered almonds and raisins, then add the vegetables with their liquid and cover with the rest of the rice.

Put the lid on the Römertopf, put on the middle shelf of a cold oven, turn the oven to 200°C (180°C fan) 400°F, gas 6 and cook for about 1 hour.

If you do not have a Römertopf, use a baking dish sealed closely with aluminium foil.

Take the Römertopf out of the oven, stir the biryani and serve, garnished with the eggs and lime wedges.

Lentil soup

Prep and cook time: 1 hour 20 minutes
Can be frozen
Serves: 4

Ingredients:
200 g | 1 cup green lentils, washed
100 g | ½ cup red lentils, washed
100 g | ½ cup brown lentils, washed
50 g | ¼ cup black beans
30 g | ⅓ cup onion, finely diced
30 g | ⅓ cup celery, finely diced
30 g | ⅓ cup carrot, finely diced
1500 ml | 6 cups vegetable stock
1 tsp finely ground cumin
2 tsp lemon zest
3 tomatoes, peeled, seeds removed, finely chopped
1 tbsp sesame paste (tahini)
1 tbsp tomato puree
garam masala, to taste
1 pinch sugar
1 tbsp green curry powder

For the yoghurt dressing:
300 g yoghurt
100 ml | 7 tbsp cream, whipped
¼ cucumber, peeled, seeds removed, half cut into sticks, half grated
1 red bell pepper, seeds removed, diced
1 garlic clove, crushed

Method:

Simmer the lentils, beans, onion, celery and carrot in the stock with the cumin for 40-50 minutes.

To make the yoghurt dressing, place the yoghurt in a bowl and add the whipped cream. Squeeze the juice out of the grated cucumber and add to the yoghurt. Stir in the bell pepper and the garlic. Season with salt and pour into glasses garnished with the cucumber sticks.

Add the lemon zest, tomatoes, sesame paste (tahini) and the tomato puree to the lentils and bring to a boil. Season with the garam masala, salt, ground black pepper, a pinch of sugar, and the curry powder. Re-heat and serve in preheated bowls.

Serve with the yoghurt and add to the soup as desired.

Potato dhal

Prep and cook time: 55 minutes
Cannot be frozen
Serves: 4

Ingredients:
250 g | 1 ⅓ cups red lentils, washed
1 tsp turmeric
1 tsp Cayenne pepper
2 medium onions, finely chopped
4 garlic cloves, finely chopped
1 tsp fresh ginger, peeled and grated
4 tbsp ghee
1 tsp ground coriander
½ tsp cumin
1-2 tsp red curry paste
500-600 g | 3-4 cups
boiled potatoes, diced
2 tomatoes, roughly chopped
25 g | 1 cup fresh coriander|cilantro,
roughly chopped

Method:

Cook the lentils in pot with 1 ½ pints water. Add the turmeric and ½ tsp Cayenne pepper and simmer on a low heat for 10 minutes with the lid half off. The lentils should still be slightly firm. Drain.

Mix together the onions, garlic and ginger. Heat the ghee in a large skillet and fry the mixture until light brown. Add the ground coriander, cumin and the rest of the Cayenne pepper and stir in the curry paste.

Mix in the potatoes and the tomatoes. Add ¼ pint water, bring to a boil and allow to cook on a low heat for 10 minutes with the lid on.

Add the lentils and a little salt and cook for a further 5 minutes - if necessary add a little more water.

Season the potato dhal with salt and Cayenne pepper. Mix most of the coriander/cilantro into the dhal and serve immediately garnished with the remaining coriander/cilantro

Baghara baingan – aubergines in peanut sauce

Prep and cook time: 40 minutes
Cannot be frozen
Serves: 4

Ingredients:
6 tbsp oil
600 g | 1 ½ lbs small aubergines|eggplants
200 g | 1 ¾ cups peanuts, chopped
1 tbsp sesame seeds
2 tbsp desiccated coconut
1 tbsp tamarind paste
1 tsp turmeric
4 small green chilli peppers, whole
4 bay leaves

Method:

Heat 4 tbsp oil and fry the aubergines/eggplants in a skillet for a few minutes. Fry on all sides and then turn down the heat and allow them to soften.

Dry roast the peanuts and sesame seeds in another skillet. Mix in the desiccated coconut, the tamarind paste and as much water as necessary to create a thick sauce.

Add the remaining oil, turmeric, chillies and the bay leaves and cook everything on a low heat for 10 minutes. If necessary add more water. Season with salt, mix in the aubergines/eggplants and serve with rice.

Chickpea soup with rosemary

Prep and cook time: 20 minutes
Can be frozen
Serves: 4

Ingredients:
4 cloves garlic
4 tbsp olive oil
2 tsp rosemary leaves
800 ml | 3 ½ cups vegetable stock
600 g | 2 ½ cups chickpeas|garbanzo
beans, **canned**
poppadoms, to serve

Method:

Peel and thinly slice the garlic and roast in a pan in hot oil until golden brown, then remove from the pan.

Gently fry the rosemary in oil, then remove from the pan. Add the stock and the drained chickpeas/garbanzo beans and bring to the boil. Simmer for 5 minutes.

Take out about 2 ladlefuls of the chickpeas/garbanzo beans and puree the rest. Return the chickpeas/garbanzo beans to the soup, season with salt and pepper and reheat.

Serve in small bowls. Garnish with roasted garlic and rosemary and serve with poppadoms.

Suran ka salan – vegetable curry with yams

Prep and cook time: 45 minutes
Cannot be frozen
Serves: 4

Ingredients:
1000 g | 2 lbs yam, cut
into rough pieces
2 medium sweet potatoes, diced
4 tsp ghee
1 medium onion, finely sliced
2 garlic cloves, halved
1 tsp fresh grated ginger
2 cardamom pods
2 tsp sugar
1 tbsp ground coriander
1 tbsp vindaloo paste
1 tsp turmeric
½ cinnamon stick
200 g yoghurt

Method:
Cook the yams in salt water for 15 minutes until they're becoming tender. Add the sweet potatoes and simmer for a further 10 minutes. Drain and set aside.

Heat the ghee and fry the onion, garlic and ginger until golden brown. Stir in the seeds from the cardamom pod, the sugar, ground coriander, vindaloo paste, turmeric and cinnamon.

Add the yam and sweet potatoes and pour on 100 ml / ½ cup water.

Simmer for 10 minutes, stir in the yoghurt and season to taste.

Aloo mutter

Prep and cook time: 50 minutes
Can be frozen
Serves: 4

Ingredients:
3 tbsp ghee
1 tbsp panch phoron
(Indian five-spice mixture)
1 tsp garam masala
120 g | 1 $\frac{1}{5}$ cups spring
onions|scallions, cut into rings
500 g | 3 $\frac{1}{3}$ cups baking
potatoes, diced
4 carrots, diced
2 chilli peppers, seeds removed,
cut into fine strips
1 tsp fresh ginger, peeled and
finely chopped
400 ml | 1 $\frac{2}{3}$ cups vegetable stock
1 tsp turmeric
1 tsp ground cumin
300 g | 2 cups peas
2 tsp sweet paprika

Method:
Heat the ghee in a large pot and cook the panch phoron and
the garam masala until the scent becomes noticeable.

Add the spring onions/scallions and fry until transparent.
Add the potatoes, carrots, chilli and ginger and fry together on
a medium heat for 3-4 minutes, stirring occasionally.

Add the stock, turmeric and cumin. Simmer on a medium heat,
stirring often, for 20 minutes until the potatoes and carrots are
al dente. After 15 minutes add the peas.

Season with paprika, salt and ground black pepper
and serve with naan bread.

Chickpea curry

Prep and cook time: 15 minutes
Can be frozen
Serves: 4

Ingredients:
400 g | 2 cups chickpeas|garbanzo
beans, soaked overnight
2 tbsp ghee
2 garlic cloves, finely chopped
1 onion, finely chopped
250 g |1 cup canned tomatoes
1 tsp ground cumin
1 tsp curry powder
Cayenne pepper
250 g | 1 ²/₅ cup Basmati rice

To garnish:
several coriander|cilantro leaves

Method:

Cook the chickpeas/garbanzo beans in salted water for 30 minutes until almost tender. Drain.

Heat the ghee and fry the chickpeas/garbanzo beans garlic, onion, tomatoes, cumin, curry and Cayenne pepper. Simmer everything for 20 minutes until almost all the liquid has evaporated.

Cook the rice according to the directions on the packet.

Season the curry with salt. Serve, garnished with coriander/cilantro and rice.

Vegetable dahl with coconut

Prep and cook time: 45 minutes
Can be frozen
Serves: 4

Ingredients:
4 tbsp ghee
1 tsp ground turmeric
1 pinch chilli powder
1/2 tsp ground cumin
1 tsp garam masala
300 g | 1 1/2 cups yellow lentils,
washed and drained
4 fresh bay leaves
1 tsp mustard seeds
500 g | 4 cups mixed vegetables
2 tbsp desiccated coconut
poppadoms, to serve

Method:

Heat 2 tbsp ghee in a pot and cook the turmeric, chilli, cumin and garam masala. Stir in the lentils and then add 850 ml / 1 1/2 pints water.

Allow to cook on a medium heat for 25-30 minutes with a lid on, stirring occasionally until the dhal becomes thick.
Add a little more water and season with salt.

Heat the remaining ghee and quickly fry the bay leaves and mustard seeds with a lid on. Caution: the mustard seeds pop!

Add the vegetables and fry until golden brown. Add a little water and cook for 5 minutes until al dente. Season with salt and ground black pepper.

Arrange the dhal in bowls, place the vegetables on top and garnish with desiccated coconut. Serve with poppadoms.

rice & bread.

Pilau rice

Prep and cook time: 30 minutes
Cannot be frozen
Serves: 4

Ingredients:
200 g | 1 ¼ cups rice, washed, drained
1 onion, finely chopped
40 g | ¼ cup butter
400 ml | 1 ⅔ cups chicken stock

To garnish:
1 large onion, sliced in rings
2 tbsp ghee
1-2 tsp icing|confectioners' sugar

Method:

Heat the oven to 200°C (180°C fan) 400°F, gas 6.

Fry the onions in ghee until transparent. Add the rice and stir until glassy. Pour in the hot chicken stock and season with salt to taste. Cover and place in the oven. Cook for 20 minutes.

For the garnish, fry the onion rings in ghee until golden brown. Sprinkle with icing/confectioners' sugar and let caramelize slightly. Serve on the rice.

Lamb biryani

Prep and cook time: 1 hour 50 minutes
Can be frozen
Serves: 4

Ingredients:
100 ml | 7 tbsp milk
½ tsp saffron threads
400 g | 2 ⅓ cups Basmati rice
6 cardamom pods
½ stick cinnamon
1 bay leaf
5 cloves
5 tbsp ghee
4 onions, 3 chopped, 1 sliced
in half rings
1 tsp turmeric
2 tbsp ground coriander
1 tbsp ground cumin
1 tsp chilli powder
2 tbsp ginger, peeled and grated
2 tbsp garlic, crushed
3 tomatoes, skinned, chopped
500 g yoghurt
200 g | 1 ⅓ cup peas, thawed if frozen
100 g | ½ cup raisins
1000 g | 2 lbs lamb, loin, fat removed,
meat chopped into bite-size pieces
2 green chilli peppers, chopped
2 tsp garam masala
50 g | ¼ cup butter

To serve:
flaked|slivered almonds

Method:
Heat the oven to 180°C (160°C fan) 375°F, gas 5.

Warm the milk and let the saffron soften in the milk.
Soak the rice in cold water for 30 minutes.

Drain the rice and cook with the cinnamon, bay leaf,
cardamom and cloves in salted water until ¾ done.
Drain well in a sieve.

Heat the ghee in a large oven-proof pan with a heavy lid.
Fry the chopped onions in the ghee. Add all the ground spices
except the garam masala, stirring all the time. Fry for
30 seconds. If the mixture is too dry, add a little more ghee.
Add the ginger and garlic and fry for a further 30 seconds.

Add the tomatoes and continue to fry, stirring, until the oil
separates from the mixture. The tomatoes should disintegrate
and all ingredients merge to an even, soft consistency.

Turn the heat up to high. Gradually add half the yoghurt; stir in
the peas and raisins. Stir well. Add the meat, season with salt
and simmer until the meat is done.

Fry the onion rings separately in oil and drain on kitchen paper.
Stir the chopped chillies into the sauce. Take half the meat and
sauce out of the pan. Cover the meat and sauce in the pan
with half the rice.

Sprinkle over 1 tsp garam masala, half the fried onions and half
the saffron milk. Add the butter in pieces. Repeat the layers
with the remaining half of the ingredients.

Cover and place in the oven for 20 minutes.

Garnish with flaked/slivered almonds to serve.

Idli sambar – steamed rice cakes with Indian stew

Prep and cook time: 1 hour Waiting time: 10 hours
Cannot be frozen
Serves: 4

Ingredients:
For the idli:
300 g | 3 cups ravva rice
200 g | 1 cup Urad Dhal
(split black gram)
1 tbsp oil

For the sambar:
200 g | 1 cup arahar (toor dhal),
washed and soaked in water for ½ hour.
1 tsp fenugreek (methi) seeds
1 tsp red chilli powder
½ tsp coriander powder
½ tsp cumin seeds
¼ tsp coriander seeds
1 pinch asafoetida powder
½ tsp mustard seeds
1 tsp oil
½ carrot, chopped into chunks
5 green chillies, chopped
5 okra, chopped into chunks
3 small aubergine|eggplant, chopped
into chunks
1 tomato, chopped
2 cm | ½ in fresh ginger, peeled
and chopped
25 g | 1 cup coriander|cilantro leaves
8 curry leaves
1 tbsp lime juice
1 tsp tamarind, soaked in water
and crushed
900 ml | 4 cups | water

Method:
For the idli:

Wash the rice ravva. Soak in water for 8-10 hours.

Wash the dhal. Soak in water for 8-10 hours.

Drain all the water from the dhal and blend to a thick paste.

Drain all the water from the rice ravva and add to the dhal paste. Add salt to taste (about 1 tsp). Mix well.

Transfer the mixture to a deep skillet (it should not be more than half full. If your skillet is too small, divide the mixture between 2 skillets). Cover the skillet with a plate and set in a warm place for 8-10 hours to let the mixture ferment. The mixture will rise and fill the skillet.

Grease idli plates with the oil and fill with the mixture. Cook for about 10 minutes.

For the sambar:

Place the dhal in a pressure cooker and add 2 cups of water. Cook for about 8-10 minutes after the pressure is reached.

Heat the fenugreek seeds in a frying pan until they turn dark. Remove the seeds and let them cool. Grind in a blender to make powder.

Heat 2 tsp oil in a deep skillet. Add cumin seeds and fry over a medium heat. When the seeds pop, add all the spices including the fenugreek powder. Fry briefly and then add all the vegetables including coriander/cilantro leaves and curry leaves. Stir and fry for 2-3 minutes. Add 475 ml / 2 cups water. Boil for 10 minutes.

Add the dhal and mix well.

Serve the idli and sambar hot.

Carrot, apricot and raisin pilau

Prep and cook time: 1 hour
Cannot be frozen
Serves: 4

Ingredients:
1 onion, peeled and chopped
20 g | 1 tbsp butter
2 cardamom pods, halved
1 stick cinnamon
4 cloves
300 g | 2 cups Basmati rice
700 ml | 3 cups water
$\frac{1}{2}$ tsp saffron threads
$\frac{1}{2}$ tsp pepper
1 large carrot, cut into thin sticks
4 tbsp almonds, or cashew nuts, chopped
4 tbsp raisins
5 dried apricots, sliced into strips

Method:
Fry the onion in butter until soft. Add the cardamom pods, the cinnamon stick and the cloves and continue to fry for 2-3 minutes.

Add the rice and fry until transparent. Pour on 700 ml / 3 cups water. Dissolve the saffron in 1 tbsp hot water, season with pepper and add.

Add the carrot, half the almonds, the raisins and the apricots. Bring to a boil and simmer for 40 minutes over a low heat until done.

Season with sea salt and serve, garnished with the remaining chopped almonds.

Biryani

Prep and cook time: 15 minutes
Cannot be frozen
Serves: 4

Ingredients:
50 g | ¼ cup raisins
4 cardamom pods
2 cloves
1 pinch saffron powder
¼ tsp cinnamon
250 g | 2 cups Basmati rice
50 g | ½ cup flaked|slivered almonds
1 lime, juiced

To garnish:
lime slices
cinnamon stick

Method:

Soften the raisins in lukewarm water.

Boil 500 ml / 1 pint water seasoned with salt, ground black pepper, the cardamom pods, cloves, saffron and cinnamon. Then add the rice and simmer for 15 minutes with a lid on. Remove from the heat and allow to soak for a further 10 minutes.

Dry roast the almonds and mix into the rice along with the lime juice and the raisins. Season with salt and pepper and serve garnish with lime slices and cinnamon sticks.

Saffron rice with almonds and raisins

Prep and cook time: 35 minutes
Cannot be frozen
Serves: 4

Ingredients:
3 tbsp ghee
40 g | ½ cup flaked|slivered almonds
4 cardamom pods
3 cloves
1/2 cinnamon stick
300 g | 1 ½ cups Basmati rice
1 pinch saffron threads
40 g | ⅓ cup raisins
2 tbsp lime juice
1 tsp salt

To garnish:
4 sprigs parsley

Method:

Heat the ghee and sauté the flaked/slivered almonds, cardamom, cloves and cinnamon, stir continuously.

Add the rice and sauté briefly. Add the saffron and 600 ml / 2 ½ cups water. Bring to the boil, cover and cook very gently over a very low heat for 20 minutes.

Soak the raisins in a little lukewarm water and 5 minutes before the end of cooking time, carefully stir the raisins into the rice.

Season to taste with lime juice and salt. Garnish with sprigs of parsley and serve immediately.

Idli – rice cakes

Prep and cook time: 40 minutes
Can be frozen
Serves: 4 (12 idli)

Ingredients:
1 tbsp ghee, or oil
½ tsp mustard seeds
1 tbsp channa dhal, (split lentils)
3 green chillies, finely chopped
1 tsp fresh ginger, peeled and grated
250 ml | 1 cups sooji ravva
(semolina|cream of wheat)
1 pinch soda
2 carrots, grated
50 g | ¼ cup raisins
2 tbsp grated fresh coconut
225 ml | 1 cup | 1 cup thick curd,
well beaten
2 tbsp roasted cashew nuts

To garnish:
coriander/cilantro leaves

Method:
Heat ghee, add the mustard seeds and once they splutter, add the chana dhal and sauté until the dhal turns golden brown. Add the green chillies and ginger.

Immediately add the sooji ravva and stir fry on low to medium heat, stirring constantly for 3 minutes. Take off the heat and cool.

Add the soda, grated carrot, raisins, grated coconut, curd, 50 ml / ¼ cup water and salt and mix well. Let it stand for at least half an hour.

Grease idli plates. Place a roasted cashew nut on each of the greased idli plates and pour the batter over the cashew nut. Don't let the batter fill to the brim.

Steam the idlis on medium flame for 10 minutes. Turn off heat and let it sit for 5 minutes. Remove the idlis carefully with a spatula and chop. Garnish with coriander/cillantro and serve hot with chutney of your choice.

Vegetable rice

Prep and cook time: 40 minutes
Cannot be frozen
Serves: 4

Ingredients:
8 strands saffron
50 g | ½ cup cashew nuts, chopped
1 stick cinnamon
6 pods cardamom
4 cloves
2 bay leaves
2 tbsp ghee
1 carrot, cut in fine strips
250 g | 1 ½ cups Basmati rice
2 tbsp raisins
100 g | ¼ lb cauliflower florets
100 g | ⅔ cup frozen peas
100 g | ¼ lb green|string beans,
cut into small pieces
500 ml | 2 cups vegetable stock
1 tsp sugar

Method:
Soak the saffron in 2 tbsp hot water.

Roast the cashew nuts with the cinnamon, the cardamom, the cloves and the bay leaves one after the other in a skillet without fat until they give off an aroma. Take out of the skillet.

Heat the ghee in the skillet. Fry the carrot and rice quickly. Add the nuts, the roasted spices, the raisins, cauliflower, beans, peas and soaked saffron. Pour in the vegetable stock and season with salt and sugar.

Bring to a boil, cover and cook over a low heat for 18 minutes. The rice should soak up the liquid. Season with salt and pepper.

Chapatis with cucumber and mint raita

Prep and cook time: 45 minutes Resting time: 1 hour
Cannot be frozen
Serves: 4

Ingredients:
For the chapatis:
300 g | 2 ⅓ cup plain|all purpose flour
1 tbsp ghee

For the cucumber and mint raita:
400 g yoghurt
½ tsp salt
¼ tsp Cayenne pepper
½ cucumber, peeled and grated
2 tbsp mint leaves, finely chopped

To garnish:
mint leaves

Method:

For the chapatis, put the flour into a bowl and gradually knead in 150 ml / ⅔ cup lukewarm water. Transfer the dough to a lightly floured work surface and continue to knead for about 10 minutes until soft. Then wrap in foil or cling film and leave to rest for 1 hour.

Form the dough into a roll and divide into 12 portions. On a lightly floured work surface roll out each portion to a circle approximately 15 cm / 6" in diameter.

Rub a frying pan with ghee and cook each chapati on both sides over a medium heat until small brown flecks appear.

For the raita, stir the yoghurt until smooth, then stir in the salt and Cayenne pepper. Fold in the cucumber and mint. Spoon into small bowls and garnish with mint.

Naan bread with a spicy potato filling

Prep and cook time: 4 hours 35 minutes
Cannot be frozen
Serves: 4

Ingredients:
250 g | 2 cups flour
3 ½ g | 1 tsp easy bake yeast
1 tsp sugar
½ tsp salt
1 tbsp oil
50 g | ¼ cup yoghurt
2 tbsp black sesame seeds

For the filling:
2 tbsp ghee
25 g | 1 cup spring onions|scallions,
finely chopped
600 g 4 cups potatoes, diced
1 scotch bonnet or tabasco chilli
pepper, finely chopped
150 ml | ⅝ cup vegetable stock

Method:
Heat the oven to 220°C (200°C fan) 425°F, gas 7.

Mix the flour and the yeast in a bowl. Add the sugar, salt, oil, yoghurt and 75 ml / 6 tbsp lukewarm water and knead into a soft dough. If necessary use a little more or a little less water. Cover and allow to rise for 30 minutes.

Heat the ghee and sweat the spring onions/scallions. Add the potatoes, chilli and 2 tbsp of the stock. Season with salt and simmer for 15 minutes with a lid on until the potatoes are al dente. Add extra stock as and when required, but make sure there is no water left at the end. Let cool.

Re-knead the dough thoroughly, divide into quarters and roll out into four rounds.

Place the filling in the middle and fold the dough in half. Press the edges closed with a fork. Sprinkle with sesame seeds and bake in the preheated oven for 15-20 minutes until golden brown.

Sada dosa – ground rice flatbread

Prep and cook time: 40 minutes Soaking: 12 hours Standing: 12 hours
Cannot be frozen
Serves: 4

Ingredients:
100 g | ½ cups Urid Dahl (Indian lentils)
300 g | 2 cups patna rice
1 tbsp boiled rice
1 tsp fenugreek
1 pinch salt
oil, for cooking

Method:
Soak the rice and lentils separately overnight in plenty of water. Drain them next morning, saving the soaking water.

Place the drained rice in a blender. Add the boiled rice and blend on the highest setting. Add just enough of the soaking liquid to make a smooth paste.

Puree the lentils to a fine paste with a little of the soaking liquid, too. Add the fenugreek.

Mix the two pastes. Add salt and let stand in a warm place overnight.

In the morning the mixture should taste slightly sour and be fairly liquid. Stir in a little more water if necessary.

Heat a little oil in a pan and pour in a little of the dough. Tip the pan to spread the dough evenly and cook at medium heat. After 1-2 minutes, when the surface is nearly dry, turn the flatbread over and cook the other side.

Bake the remaining flatbreads in the same way. The quantity is enough for 8-12 flatbreads, depending on the pan size. Keep warm until ready to serve.

Paratha

Prep and cook time: 30 minutes
Can be frozen
Serves: 4

Ingredients:
5 tbsp ghee
250 g | 2 cups whole grain flour
50 g | 1/3 cup roti flour, or
plain|all purpose flour
1/2 tsp sea salt
a little ghee, for frying

Method:

Melt 3 tbsp of the ghee. Place both kinds of flour in a large bowl and make a dip in the centre. Pour the sea salt, 125 ml / 2/3 cup water and the melted ghee into the dip and knead well (1-2 tbsp water may be added if necessary). The dough should remain soft. Cover the dough and let rest for 1 hour.

Divide the dough into 6-8 pieces. Roll out each piece, on a floured surface, to a thin circle. Place the circles next to each other. Melt 2 tbsp ghee and rub it into the dough circles.

Melt a little ghee in a pan and cook the parathas for 2-3 minutes.

Appam kerala – rice and coconut flatbread

Prep and cook time: 1 hour 10 minutes
Can be frozen
Serves: 4

Ingredients:
2 tbsp semolina|cream of wheat
200 g | 2 cups rice flour
1 tsp easy bake yeast
2 tbsp caster|superfine sugar
175 ml | ¾ cup | 1 cup coconut milk
ghee, for frying

To garnish:
spices, to taste

Method:

Bring 475 ml / 16 fl oz / 2 cups water to a boil and stir in the semolina/cream of wheat. Boil until thickened, stirring continuously. Take off the heat and let cool.

Mix the rice flour with the yeast, sugar, cooled semolina paste and mix to a smooth dough. Add enough water to give the dough a thick pouring consistency. Allow it to stand for 20 minutes.

Heat the ghee in a skillet and fry the dough in portions (like pancakes). Garnish with spices to serve.

Puri bread with mango sauce

Prep and cook time: 1 hour
Cannot be frozen
Serves: 4

Ingredients:
250 g | 2 cups whole wheat flour
100 ml | 7 tbsp vegetable oil
$^1/_2$ tsp salt

For the sauce:
400 ml | 1 $^2/_3$ cups | 1 $^1/_2$ cups canned mango pulp
1 pinch chilli powder
1 pinch ground ginger

Method:

Place the flour in a bowl and slowly add 175 ml / $^3/_4$ cup warm water. Knead to a soft dough. Cover the bowl and leave to rise for at least 30 minutes.

Knead again thoroughly. Form the dough into small balls and roll these out to 15 cm / 6" circles.

Heat the oil in a pan and add a little salt. Place a puri circle in the pan and press it under the oil until it expands. Then turn and fry very quickly on the other side. Drain on kitchen paper.

For the mango sauce, mix the mango pulp with the spices. Serve the puri hot with the mango sauce.

Crispy flatbread with rosemary

Prep and cook time: 1 hour 40 minutes
Cannot be frozen
Serves: 4

Ingredients:
10 g | 3 tsp easy bake yeast
500 g | 4 cups plain|all purpose flour
1 tsp salt
8 tbsp olive oil
1 bunch rosemary, finely chopped
1 tbsp coarse sea salt

To garnish:
1 sprig rosemary

Method:
Sprinkle the yeast over the flour and salt. Mix in 250 ml / 1 cup lukewarm water and 5 tbsp olive oil into a bowl and knead to a pliable dough. It should not stick to the bowl. Cover and put in a warm place until it has doubled in size.

Mix the rosemary with 3 tbsp olive oil.

Turn the dough on to a floured working surface and knead, but not too heavily. Then form into a roll approximately 5 cm / 2 in depth. Now cut off equal-sized pieces with a knife and roll each one out quite thinly on plenty of flour.

Heat a large non-stick skillet (not too hot) and fry one after the other on both sides until crisp. Brush lightly with the rosemary oil and sprinkle with sea salt. Cool on a rack.

Continue in this way until all the dough is used up.

desserts.

Modak – sweet steamed dumplings

Prep and cook time: 45 minutes Rest: 1 hour
Cannot be frozen
Serves: 4

Ingredients:
250 g | 2 cups plain|all purpose flour
1 pinch salt
1 tsp easy-bake yeast
1 tbsp olive oil
2 tbsp ground almonds
1-2 tsp fine sugar
1 pinch anise seed
1 pinch cinnamon
1 tsp rose water
1-2 tbsp cream
rose petals, to garnish

Method:
In a bowl mix the flour with the salt and make a well in the middle. Mix the yeast with 200 ml / 1 cup warm water and pour into the well. Add the olive oil and knead thoroughly into a smooth dough. Cover the bowl with a towel and let the dough rise in a warm place for 1 hour until it has doubled in size.

To make the filling, mix the almonds, sugar, anise seed, cinnamon and rose water with the cream.

Re-knead the dough on a floured surface and divide into plum-size pieces. With floured hands, gently squash each piece flat and place some filling on top. Wrap the dough around the filling and shape into balls.

In a pot bring some water to a boil. Lay a cotton tea towel in a colander and place the dumplings inside but make sure they are not touching. Steam on a medium heat for 15-20 minutes with a lid on. You may have to steam the dumplings in batches.

To serve, cut a small slit in each ball and place a rose petal in the slit.

Mango lassi

Prep and cook time: 20 minutes
Can be frozen
Serves: 4

Ingredients:
1 ripe mango, flesh cut off the stone
1 banana, chopped
500 ml | 2 cups natural yoghurt
3 tbsp lemon juice
1 tsp cardamom, ground
200 ml | $^7/_8$ cup liquid honey
2 ice cubes

Method:
Put the yoghurt, 200 ml / $^3/_4$ cup water, the mango and banana into a blender and blend to a puree. Blend in the lemon juice, cardamom, honey and ice cubes.

Pour into glasses and serve.

Halva

Prep and cook time: 3 hour 20 minutes
Can be frozen
Serves: 4

Ingredients:
150 g | ³/₄ cup butter
1 large carrot, finely grated
150 g | 1 cup semolina|cream of wheat
400 ml | 1 ³/₄ cups milk
100 g | ¹/₂ cup sugar

To decorate:
edible gold foil
small paper cases

Method:

Heat the oven to 100°C (80°C fan), 200°F, very low.

Melt the butter in a pot, add the carrot and semolina/cream of wheat and cook on a low heat stirring continuously for 2 minutes.

Heat the milk and sugar in a second pot until the sugar has dissolved. Pour over the semolina-carrot mixture and stir in well.

Pour the mass into a greased cake tin 20 cm x 20 cm / 8" x 8" and bake in the oven for 3 hours. You should then be able to cut the mixture.

Knock the halva gently out of the tin and cut into small pieces. Place into paper cases and decorate with gold foil.

Peach and pear raita with cinnamon

Prep and cook time: 20 minutes
Cannot be frozen
Serves: 4

Ingredients:
2 ripe pears, peeled, cored and diced
2 ripe peaches, peeled, stones removed and diced
2 tbsp sugar
4 tbsp lemon juice
1 tsp fresh grated ginger
600 g yoghurt
50 ml | 10 tsp cream
1 tbsp liquid honey
1 tsp ground cinnamon

Method:
Mix the fruit with the sugar and 2 tbsp lemon juice.

Mix the ginger with the yoghurt, cream, honey and the remaining lemon juice. Add the fruit and serve in bowls sprinkled with cinnamon.

Pista khaja – filo pastry with a pistachio filling

Prep and cook time: 25 minutes
Cannot be frozen
Serves: 4

Ingredients:
For the syrup:
110 g | ½ cup sugar
2 - 3 tbsp lemon juice
10 saffron threads

For the filo pastry:
50 g | ½ cup ground pistachio nuts
20 g | 1 ½ tbsp sugar
½ tsp ground cardamom
1 sheet filo pastry, or
12 wonton wrappers
ghee, for frying

Method:

To make the syrup allow the sugar to caramelize in a large skillet. Add 50 ml / ¼ cup water and the lemon juice. Add the saffron threads and allow to simmer until a fine syrup is formed.

To make the filling, mix the pistachios, sugar and the cardamom. Stir into a spreadable paste by adding 6 tbsp water.

Cut the filo pastry into squares (7 x 7 cm / 3" x 3"). Spread half of each square with the pistachio paste and fold in half.

Heat the ghee in a pot and deep fry the pastry for 1-3 minutes until golden brown. Pat dry with kitchen paper.

Dip the pastry into the saffron syrup and let dry on a wire rack.

Almond kulfi with cardamom

Prep and cook time: 30 minutes Freeze: 6 hours
Can be frozen
Serves: 4

Ingredients:
400 ml | 1 ²/₃ cups sweetened condensed milk
75 ml | ¹/₃ cup whipping cream
75 g | 1 cup flaked|slivered almonds
¹/₂ tsp ground cardamom
6 saffron threads
2 drops rosewater
100 g | 2 cups spaghetti
2 tbsp icing|confectioners' sugar

To garnish:
8 saffron threads
25 g | ¹/₄ cup pistachios, chopped
1 tbsp almonds, chopped

Method:

Boil the condensed milk, 200 ml / 1 ¹/₈ cups water, cream, flaked/slivered almonds, cardamom and saffron threads then turn down the heat and allow to simmer.

Stir in the rose water and let the mixture cool. Pour into a suitable container, cover and freeze for 3 hours.

After three hours, remove from the freezer and stir with a mixer. Pour into four moulds or bowls, cover and freeze again for another 3 hours.

20 minutes before serving, cook the spaghetti according to the directions on the packet. Then drain.

Heat the butter in a large skillet. Warm the spaghetti and sprinkle with icing/confectioners' sugar.

Serve the ice cream on plates with the sweetened spaghetti. Sprinkle with saffron threads, pistachios and almonds.

Gulab jamuns – Indian pastries in syrup

Prep and cook time: 40 minutes Marinade: 30 minutes
Cannot be frozen
Serves: 4

Ingredients:
300 g | 1 ½ cups sugar
8 cardamom pods
175 g | 1 ²/₅ cups milk powder
2 tsp baking powder
50 g | ²/₅ cup flour
1 tbsp semolina|cream of wheat
150 ml | ⁵/₈ cup milk
oil, for frying
2 tbsp rose water

To garnish:
1 tbsp pistachios, chopped
untreated rose petals

Method:
To make the syrup, heat the sugar in 300 ml / 1 ¼ cups water on a medium/low heat until the sugar has dissolved. Add the cardamom pods and simmer for a further 2 minutes. Set aside.

Mix the milk powder, baking powder, flour and semolina/cream of wheat with 100 ml / ½ cup milk. Knead into a pliable dough. If necessary add a little more milk.

Divide the dough into 24 small balls and cover with a damp tea towel.

Heat the oil (it is hot enough when bubbles form on the handle of a wooden spoon dipped into the hot oil). Fry the balls for 2-4 minutes until golden brown. Remove with a draining spoon and place on kitchen paper to dry.

Add the rose water to the cool syrup. Place the fried dough balls in the syrup and steep for at least 30 minutes - if not overnight.

Serve the balls on plates with some of the syrup and garnish with pistachios and rose petals.

Almond pudding with saffron and pistachios

Prep and cook time: 25 minutes
Cannot be frozen
Serves: 4

Ingredients:
100 g | 1 cup ground almonds
400 ml | 1 ³⁄₄ cups milk
20 g | 1 tbsp semolina|cream of wheat
1 pinch ground cardamom
8 saffron threads
2 tbsp ghee
100 g | ¹⁄₂ cup sugar
20 g | ¹⁄₄ cup pistachios, roughly chopped
20 g | ¹⁄₄ cup almonds, roughly chopped

Method:

Mix the ground almonds with the milk, semolina/cream of wheat, cardamom and saffron.

Heat the ghee in a pot, add the almond-milk mixture and bring to a boil stirring continuously. Then simmer for 5 minutes, stirring continuously.

Add the sugar and allow to simmer for a further 8-10 minutes until a thick cream is formed. Stir occasionally.

Pour into dessert bowls and sprinkle with the chopped pistachios and almonds.

Besan laddoo – sweet gram flour balls

Prep and cook time: 35 minutes
Cannot be frozen
Serves: 4

Ingredients:
50 g | 2 tbsp ghee
200 g | 2 ⅔ cups gram (chick pea) flour
50 g | ¼ cup palm sugar, finely grated
150 g | 2 cups desiccated coconut
50 g | ¼ cup walnuts, chopped
¼ tsp cardamom powder
¼ tsp cinnamon powder

Method:
Heat the ghee in a pot. Add the gram flour and stir continuously for 5 minutes on the lowest heat so that the flour doesn't burn.

Add the palm sugar and cook for a further 15 minutes stirring continuously until the flour takes on a brown colour and has a slightly nutty aroma.

Add 1 tbsp water, 3 tbsp desiccated coconut, the walnuts, cardamom and cinnamon. Cook on the lowest heat for a further 5-7 minutes stirring continuously until a thick mass is formed.

Let the dough cool slightly and then with damp hands, shape into small balls and roll in the remaining coconut.

Banana fritters with coconut ice-cream

Prep and cook time: 1 hour 15 minutes
Cannot be frozen
Serves: 4

Ingredients:
coconut ice-cream:
400 ml | 1 ³/₄ cups coconut milk
100 ml | 7 tbsp cream
5 tbsp coconut syrup, or to taste
4 tbsp coconut liqueur

Banana fritters:
150 g | 1 ¼ cups plain|all purpose flour
100 g rice flour
100 ml | 7 tbsp coconut milk
1 egg white
1 tsp bicarbonate of soda
1 pinch salt
2-3 tbsp brown sugar
4 firm bananas, peeled,
halved
oil, for deep-frying

To serve:
pieces of pineapple
coconut flesh

To garnish:
4 sprigs mint

Method:

For the ice-cream, mix all of the ingredients, transfer to an ice cream maker and freeze. (If you do not have an ice-cream maker: mix the ingredients, put into a shallow container and put into the freezer. Freeze, whisking well every 30 minutes).

For the banana fritters: mix the flours and beat smoothly with 100 ml / ½ cup cold water. Stir in the rest of the ingredients (apart from the bananas). Add a little more water if the batter is too stiff.

Dip the bananas in the batter. Deep-fry in hot fat until crisp. Lift out with a skimmer or slotted spoon and drain on kitchen roll.

Serve on pieces of pineapple with coconut ice-cream and fresh coconut. Garnish with mint sprigs.

Deep-fried milk dumplings

Prep and cook time: 1 hour Chilling: 3 hours
Cannot be frozen
Serves: 4

Ingredients:
2 tbsp soft butter
200 g | 1 ³/₄ cups milk powder
125 g | 1 cup plain|all purpose flour
1 tsp baking powder
¹/₄ tsp ground cardamom
oil, for frying
300 g | 1 ¹/₂ cups sugar
2 tsp rose-water
sugar, for sprinkling

For decoration:
rose petals

Method:
Rub the butter into the milk powder using your fingers, until it resembles breadcrumbs. Mix in the flour with the baking powder and cardamom and gradually knead in sufficient water (about 400 ml / 1 ³/₄ cups) to make a very firm dough. Form into a ball, wrap in cling film and leave to rest for about 3 hours.

Break up the dough on a lightly floured work surface, sprinkle with water and form into balls. Deep-fry in oil over a medium heat for 3-4 minutes, a few balls at a time, until golden brown, then drain on absorbent kitchen paper.

Put the sugar and water into a saucepan, bring to a boil and boil for about 10 minutes until syrupy. Remove from the heat and stir in the rose-water. Soak the cooked dumplings in the warm syrup for about 30 minutes.

Serve either warm or cold, sprinkled with sugar. The dumplings may be served on a bed of rose petals.

Schmeesch

Prep and cook time: 35 minutes
Cannot be frozen
Serves: 4

Ingredients:
5 dried lilly flowers, softened in 2 tbsp
hot water for 30 minutes
4 oranges, juiced
1 tbsp maple syrup
¼ tsp cinnamon
1 pinch ground cloves
1 tsp fresh ginger, peeled and grated

Method:

Mix all the ingredients together with 750 ml / 1 ½ pints water.

Allow to steep for 30 minutes. Strain and pour into glasses.

Kulfi with pistachios

Prep and cook time: 45 minutes Freeze: 5 hours
Can be frozen
Serves: 8

Ingredients:
2000 ml | 8 cups whole milk
10 cardamom pods
4 tsbp sugar, more if desired
100 g | 1 $\frac{1}{4}$ cups almonds,
blanched and chopped
25 g | $\frac{1}{4}$ cup unsalted pistachios,
finely chopped
100 ml | 7 tbsp low-fat milk
edible silver foil, to decorate

Method:

Boil the whole milk in a pot. Reduce the heat so that the milk simmers but does not boil over. Add the cardamom pods and, stirring constantly, reduce the milk to $\frac{1}{3}$ of the original volume.

When the milk is reduced and thick, remove the cardamom pods and add the sugar and almonds. Cook for a further 2-3 minutes.

Pour the mixture into a bowl and, stirring frequently, let cool completely. Stir in $\frac{2}{3}$ of the pistachios.

Pour into an ice cream maker, or place in a bowl in the freezer and freeze for 2 hours stirring every 15 minutes.

Mix the low-fat milk with the remaining pistachios. Bring to a boil in a small pan and allow to foam well.

Place the ice cream in small bowls, pour the pistachio foam over and freeze immediately for 2-3 hours.

Decorate with silver foil to serve.

Saffron cake

Prep and cook time: 2 hours
Can be frozen
Serves: 8-10

Ingredients:
225 g | 1 cup sugar
50 g | ½ cup pistachios
50 g | ½ cup flaked|slivered almonds
butter, for greasing
200 g | 2 cups ground almonds
5 medium eggs
8 strands saffron
1 tbsp rum
200 g | 1 cup butter
50 g | ½ cup icing|confectioners
sugar
2 tsp lemon zest, grated
200 g | 2 cups desiccated coconut

For the glaze:
250 g | 2 cups icing|confectioners
sugar
2 tbsp milk
red food colouring
thin edible silver foil (optional)

Method:
Heat the oven to 170°C (150°C fan) 350°F, gas 4.

Grease a 26cm / 10" diameter cake tin with butter and sprinkle
2 tbsp ground almonds evenly in the bottom.

Boil 100 g / ½ cup sugar in 100 ml / ½ cup water and reduce to
a syrup for 10 minutes. Add the pistachios and flaked/slivered
almonds to the syrup and leave to soften.

Separate the eggs and beat the whites until they form stiff
peaks. While beating gradually add the remaining sugar.
Cover and chill.

Dissolve the saffron in the rum. Mix the butter with the egg yolk
and the icing/confectioners' sugar until a thick, light cream
forms. Add the saffron-rum mixture and the lemon zest. Stir for a
few more minutes until the cream is shiny and stiff.

Stir in the remaining ground almonds, the desiccated coconut
and egg white mix. Drain the softened nuts and carefully stir
into the dough.

Pour the mixture into the cake tin and bake in the middle of the
hot oven for 90 minutes.

Loosen the cake from the tin and let cool on a wire rack.

To make the glaze, mix the icing/confectioners' sugar with
the milk and 3-4 drops of food colouring. Spread the cake
generously with the glaze and decorate with silver foil. Allow to
rest before serving.

Aam kheer –
rice pudding with mango

Prep and cook time: 30 minutes
Cannot be frozen
Serves: 4

Ingredients:
140 g | 1 ¼ cups Basmati rice
400 ml | 1 ¾ cups milk
50 ml | 10 tsp cream
6 saffron threads
60 g | ¼ cup brown sugar
25 g | ¼ cup pistachios, chopped
50 g | ⅔ cup flaked|slivered almonds
1 tbsp raisins
1 tsp rose water
1 pinch ground cardamom
1 mango, diced

Method:

Place the rice, milk, cream and saffron threads in a pot and bring to a boil. Simmer for 10 minutes with a lid on

Stir in the sugar, pistachios, almonds, raisins, rose water and cardamom. Cook the rice for a further 10 minutes with a lid on.

Add the mango the rice and serve in bowls.

index